PORTABLE

WORKSHOP™

Basic Wood Projects
with Portable Power Tools

Store It
In Style

Credits

Group Executive Editor: Paul Currie
Project Director: Mark Johanson
Associate Creative Director: Tim Himsel
Managing Editor: Kristen Olson
Project Manager: Ron Bygness
Lead Project Designer: Jim Huntley
Editors: Mark Biscan, Steve Meyer
Editor & Technical Artist: Jon Simpson
Lead Art Director: Gina Seeling
Technical Production Editor: Greg Pluth
Project Designer: Steve Meyer

*Vice President of Photography
 & Production:* Jim Bindas
Copy Editor: Janice Cauley
Shop Supervisor: Phil Juntti
Lead Builder: John Nadeau
Builders: Troy Johnson, Rob Johnstone
Production Staff: Laura Hokkanen, Tom
 Hoops, Jeanette Moss, Gary Sandin,
 Mike Schauer, Mike Sipe, Brent Thomas,
 Kay Wethern

Creative Photo Coordinator:
 Cathleen Shannon
Studio Manager: Marcia Chambers
Lead Photographer: Rex Irmen
Contributing Photographer: Rebecca
 Schmitt
Photography Assistant: Dan Cary
Production Manager: Stasia Dorn
Printed on American paper by:
 Inland Press (0696)

CY DeCOSSE INCORPORATED

A COWLES MAGAZINES COMPANY

Chairman/CEO: Philip L. Penny
Chairman Emeritus: Cy DeCosse
President/COO: Nino Tarantino
Executive V.P./Editor-in-Chief:
 William B. Jones

Created by: The editors of Cy DeCosse
 Incorporated, in cooperation with Black
 & Decker. ●BLACK&DECKER is a trademark
 of the Black & Decker Corporation and
 is used under license.

Library of Congress
Cataloging-in-Publication Data

Store it in style.
        p. cm.—(Portable Workshop)
    At head of title: Black & Decker
ISBN   0-86573-683-9 (hardcover).

1. Cabinetwork. 2. Storage in the home
I. Cy DeCosse Incorporated
II. Series.
TT197.S85 1996
684.1' 8—dc20   96-15850
                                  CIP

Contents

Introduction

Household storage is one of those persistent problems that never seems to go away. No matter how many milk crates and cardboard file boxes we buy, there is always one more item that just won't fit and, after a while, everyone gets a little tired of trying. What's needed is a permanent solution, and that's where *Store It In Style* comes in. This book is filled with attractive, durable furnishings that meet specific storage and organizational needs. Years after the wire closet organizer you bought at a discount store is shipped off to the landfill, the projects you build from this book will still be rooted throughout your home, keeping the clutter at bay—and looking terrific in the process.

Is your basement or garage littered with old paint cans, brushes and roller sleeves? Turn a few 2 × 4s and a sheet of plywood into a paint center with built-in can racks and a cleanup area (see pages 74 to 79). Have soccer balls, skates and golf clubs turned your home into an obstacle course? Build a roomy sports locker with ventilated doors (see pages 8 to 11). Do you pine for a single source that can help you solve all of your most pressing storage dilemmas, without making your house look like an office supply store? You'll find what you're looking for in *Store It In Style*, a creative new project book from the Black & Decker® *Portable Workshop™*.

This book contains 20 clever household storage projects that you can build without a fancy workshop or a lot of experience working with wood. For each of the projects, you will find a complete cutting list, a lumber-shopping list, a detailed construction drawing, full-color photographs of major steps, and clear, easy-to-follow directions that guide you through every step of the project.

The Black & Decker® *Portable Workshop™* series gives weekend do-it-yourselfers the power to build beautiful wood projects. Ask your local bookseller for information on other volumes in this innovative new series.

Organizing Your Worksite

Portable power tools and hand tools offer a level of convenience that is a great advantage over stationary power tools. But using them safely and conveniently requires some basic housekeeping. Whether you are working in a garage, a basement or outdoors, it is important that you establish a flat, dry holding area where you can store tools. Set aside a piece of plywood on sawhorses, or dedicate an area of your workbench for tool storage, and be sure to return tools to that area once you are finished with them. It is also important that all waste, including lumber scraps and sawdust, be disposed of in a timely fashion. Check with your local waste disposal department before throwing away any large scraps of building materials or any finishing-material containers.

Safety Tips
•*Always wear eye and hearing protection when operating power tools and performing any other dangerous activities.*
•*Choose a well-ventilated work area when cutting or shaping wood and when using finishing products.*

Tools & Materials

At the start of each project, you will find a set of symbols that show which power tools are used to complete the project as it is shown (see below). You will also need a set of basic hand tools: a hammer, screwdrivers, tape measure, a level, a combination square, C-clamps, and pipe or bar clamps. You also will find a shopping list of all the construction materials you will need. Miscellaneous materials and hardware are listed with the cutting list that accompanies the construction drawing. When buying lumber, note that the "nominal" size of the lumber is usually larger than the "actual size." For example, a 2 × 4 is actually 1½ × 3½".

Power Tools You Will Use

Circular saw *to make straight cuts. For long cuts and rip-cuts, use a straight-edge guide. Install a carbide-tipped combination blade for most projects.*

Drills: *use a cordless drill for drilling pilot holes and counterbores, and to drive screws; use an electric drill for sanding and grinding tasks.*

Jig saw *for making contoured cuts and internal cuts. Use a combination wood blade for most projects where you will cut pine, cedar or plywood.*

Power sander *to prepare wood for a finish and to smooth out sharp edges. Owning several power sanders (⅓-sheet, ¼-sheet, and belt) is helpful.*

Belt sander *for resurfacing rough wood. Can also be used as a stationary sander when mounted on its side on a flat worksurface.*

Router *to cut decorative edges and roundovers in wood. As you gain more experience, use routers for cutting grooves (like dadoes) to form joints.*

Guide to Building Materials Used in This Book

•Sheet goods:
AB PLYWOOD: A high-grade plywood usually made from pine or fir. The better (A) side is sanded and free from knots and other defects that require filling. Moderately expensive.
BIRCH PLYWOOD: A highly workable, readily available alternative to pine or fir plywood. Has a very smooth surface that is excellent for painting or staining, and generally has fewer voids in the edges that require filling. Moderately expensive.
MDF (MEDIUM-DENSITY FIBERBOARD): Plywood with a pressed wood core that is well suited for shaping. Moderately inexpensive.
CLAD PARTICLEBOARD: Particleboard with a glossy, polymerized surface that is water-resistant and easy to clean. Inexpensive.
HARDBOARD: Basically, dense cardboard with a hard surface. Sold in ⅛ and ¼" thickness. Good for making back panels and other nonstructural parts. Very inexpensive.
PEGBOARD: Perforated hardboard.

•Dimension lumber:
PINE: A basic softwood used for many interior projects. "Select" and "#2 or better" are suitable grades. Relatively inexpensive.
RED OAK: A common hardwood that stains well and is very durable. Relatively inexpensive.
PREGLUED OAK PANELS: Wide shelf-style boards manufactured by edge-gluing strips of oak. Good for projects that require solid hardwood that is more than 9" wide. Moderate.
ASPEN: A softwood that is smooth-surfaced and workable, and sold in thicknesses of ¾" or less. Moderate.

Guide to Fasteners & Adhesives Used in This Book

•Fasteners & hardware:
WOOD SCREWS: Brass or steel; most projects use screws with a #6 or #8 shank. Can be driven with a power driver.
NAILS & BRADS: Finish nails can be set below the wood surface: common (box) nails have wide, flat heads; brads or wire nails are very small, thin fasteners with small heads.
Misc.: Door pulls & knobs; butt hinges & utility hinges; bullet catches; magnetic touch latches; carriage bolts; Lazy Susan turntable, threaded rods; other specialty hardware as indicated.

•Adhesives:
POOD GLUE: Yellow glue is suitable for all projects in this book.
PANEL ADHESIVE: Sold in cartridges for attaching sheet goods.

Finishing Your Project

Before applying finishing materials like stain or paint, fill all nail holes and blemishes with wood putty or filler. Also, fill all voids in the edges of any exposed plywood with wood putty. Sand the dried putty smooth. Alternative: fill counterbored pilot holes with wood plugs if applying stain. Sand wood surfaces with medium-grit sandpaper (80- to 120-grit), then finish-sand with fine sandpaper (150- to 180-grit). Wipe clean, then apply at least two coats of paint (enamel paint is most durable), or apply stain and at least two topcoats (water-based polyurethane is a good choice).

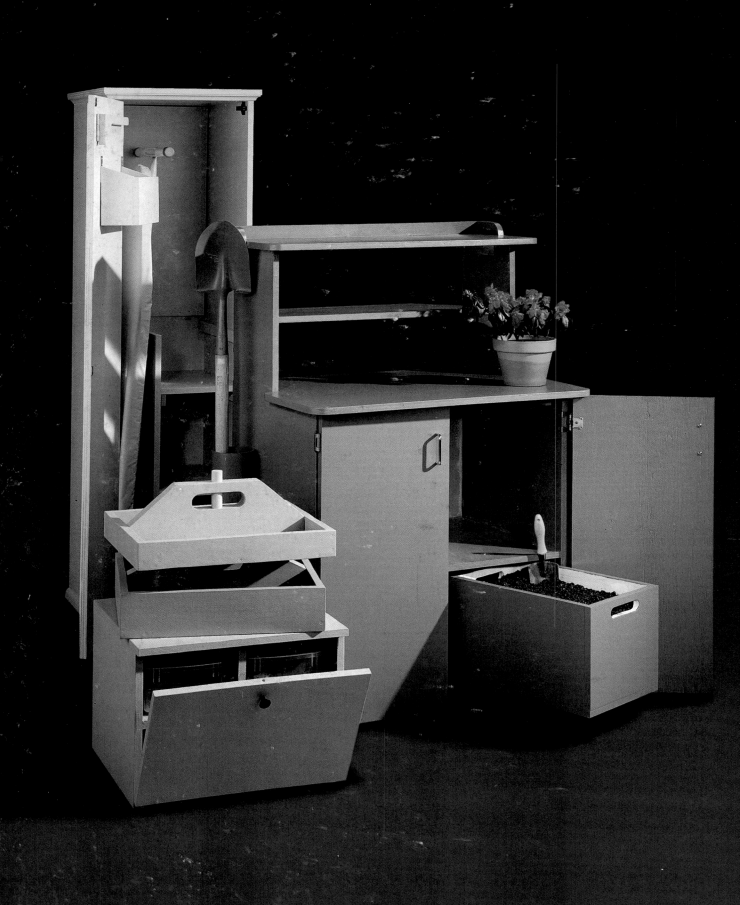

Sports Locker

Whether your game is basketball, skiing, golf, hockey, baseball or cricket, this roomy sports locker will become a most valuable project.

If you or your children are active in sports like golf, baseball, hockey or basketball, then you can imagine how valuable a good sports locker can be. Six feet tall and broad in the shoulders, this locker can handle just about anything you throw at it. But don't be afraid that this storage project will make your house smell like a locker room—the pegboard doors provide plenty of ventilation inside the locker.

If, like most people, your interest in sports is confined to a few activities, you can easily customize this sports locker to meet your needs. Add extra shelves to store more smaller-scale equipment or outdoor clothing; if you play a lot of softball, put an extra row of bat hangers in the open side; if you are an outdoorsman, replace the bat hangers with a piece of closet rod so you can store your hunting or fishing apparel in one location (where it won't pass its outdoorsy fragrance along to your other outerwear); if your family enjoys golf, eliminate the bottom two shelves to create space for two more sets of clubs. By using a little imagination, you can turn this versatile project into a real team player.

CONSTRUCTION MATERIALS

Quantity	Lumber
2	¾" × 4 × 8' plywood
1	¼" × 4 × 8' plywood
1	2 × 4" × 6' pine
6	1 × 2" × 6' pine
1	⅛" × 4 × 8' pegboard
4	½ × 1⅛" × 8' wainscot cap

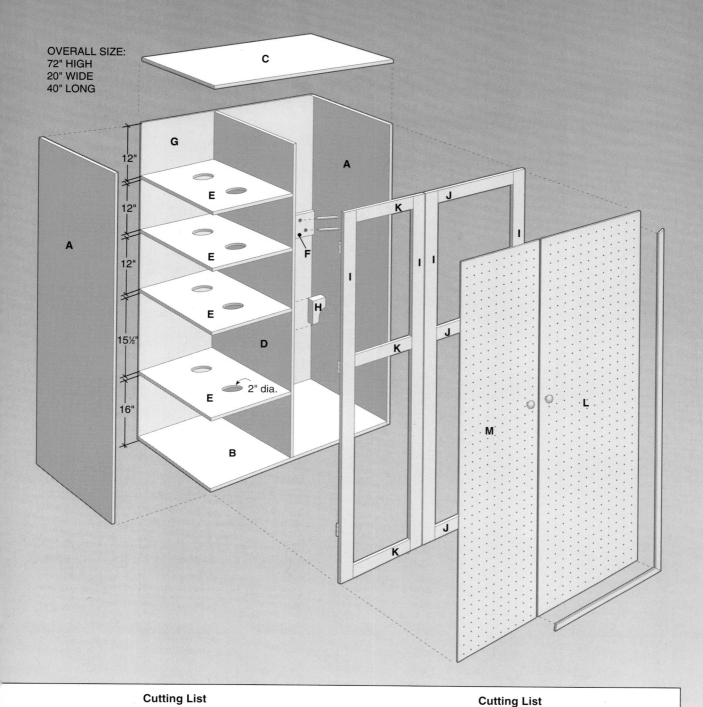

OVERALL SIZE:
72" HIGH
20" WIDE
40" LONG

2" dia.

Cutting List

Key	Part	Dimension	Pcs.	Material
A	Side	¾ × 20 × 71¼"	2	Plywood
B	Bottom	¾ × 20 × 38½"	1	Plywood
C	Top	¾ × 20 × 40"	1	Plywood
D	Divider	¾ × 20 × 70¾"	1	Plywood
E	Shelf	¾ × 16 × 20"	4	Plywood
F	Stretcher	¾ × 6 × 21¾"	1	Plywood
G	Back	¼ × 40 × 72"	1	Plywood

Cutting List

Key	Part	Dimension	Pcs.	Material
H	Hanger	1½ × 3½ × 4"	8	Pine
I	Door stile	¾ × 1½ × 71¼"	4	Pine
J	Long rail	¾ × 1½ × 19¾"	3	Pine
K	Short rail	¾ × 1½ × 14¼"	3	Pine
L	Wide door	⅛ × 22¼ × 71¼"	1	Pegboard
M	Narrow door	⅛ × 16⅜ × 71¼"	1	Pegboard

Materials: Glue, 1⅛" wainscot cap molding (32'), wood screws (#6 × 2", #8 × ¾"), 1" wire nails, 1½ × 2" butt hinges (4), door pulls or handles (2), magnetic door catches (4), Shaker-style pegs (8), finishing materials.

Note: Measurements reflect the actual size of dimensional lumber.

Install the divider panel between the top and bottom panels, separating the locker into an open area and a shelf area.

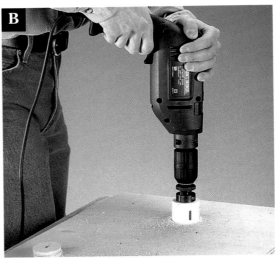

Using a hole saw, cut 2"-dia. holes in the shelves to keep balls from rolling inside the locker.

Use wood spacers to support each shelf while you fasten it with screws.

Directions: Sports Locker

BUILD THE FRAME. The sports locker is basically a plywood box with a divider panel and shelves. Start by cutting the components of the box: the sides (A), bottom (B) and top (C) from ¾"-thick plywood.

Sand the surfaces with medium (100- or 120-grit) sandpaper to smooth-out the rough spots, then fasten the bottom between the sides with glue and #6 × 2" wood screws. Counterbore the pilot holes for the screws deep enough to fill with wood putty to cover the screw heads. Attach the top to the sides with glue and screws driven down through the top and into the top edges of the side panels. Cut the divider (D) to size. Lay the box you've assembled on its back edge, and fasten the divider between the top and bottom panels of the box, 16" from the right side panel **(photo A).** Make sure the back and front edges of the divider are flush with the edges of the top and bottom panels.

BUILD THE SHELVES. Our project has four shelves, but if you prefer you may customize your sports locker to match your storage needs by adding shelves or rearranging their positions. Cut the shelves (E) to size. Because we wanted this sports locker to be able to store balls without having them roll all over the locker, we used a

2"-dia. hole saw mounted on an electric drill to drill holes in the shelves. When set in the holes, round objects remain stationary. Cut two holes in each shelf, centered from side to side, with centerpoints 5" from the front and back shelf edges **(photo B).** When using a hole saw, place a piece of scrap wood under the project to prevent damage to your worksurface. Smooth out the edges on the shelves, and sand any rough surfaces.

ATTACH THE SHELVES & BACK. Mark the shelf locations on the side and divider (see Diagram, page 9). Cut four scraps of wood the same length as the shelf height to use as spacers to support each shelf while you install it. Install the shelves by driving #6 × 2" screws through the left side and the divider, and into the edges of the shelves **(photo C).** Cut the back (G) to size. Fasten it to the sides, top and bottom with evenly spaced 1" wire nails. Nail along one side first, then square the frame before nailing the remaining edges.

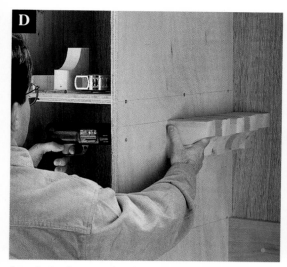

Attach the hangers by driving screws through the divider and into the ends of the hangers.

Assemble the rails and stiles to make the two different-size door frames.

ATTACH THE STRETCHER. The stretcher fits at the back of the open section of the sports locker to fortify the side-to-side strength and provide a mounting surface for pegs. Cut the stretcher (F) to size from ¾" plywood. Drill holes for Shaker-style pegs in the stretcher, making sure the holes match the diameter of the pegs. We installed two staggered rows of pegs at 8" intervals. Mark a horizontal reference line for positioning the top of the stretcher, 39" up from the bottom panel. Attach the stretcher with wood screws driven through the side and divider panels, and into the ends of the stretcher.

ATTACH THE HANGERS. We installed two rows of 2 × 4 hangers that are designed to store everything from baseball bats to canoe paddles. Cut 8 hangers (H) to size from 2 × 4 pine. Set the legs of a compass to a 2" radius, and position the point of the compass at one corner of each hanger. Draw a ¼-round cutting line at the corner, then cut along the line with a jig saw. Sand the cut

smooth. Draw reference lines for two rows of hangers 30" and 52" up from the bottom panel. Space the hangers so they are 1¼" apart—a good distance for hanging bats or paddles between the hangers. Fasten the pieces by driving two screws through the divider and into each hanger **(photo D).**

BUILD THE DOORS. The two locker doors are sized so the gap where they meet falls over the divider panel. Cut the door stiles (I), long rails (J) and short rails (K) from 1 × 2 pine. Cut the wide door (L) and narrow door (M) to size from ⅛"-thick pegboard. Apply glue to the ends of the rails, and fasten the rails between the stiles by driving wood screws through the stiles and into the rails **(photo E),** completing the door frames. Position the pegboard panels over the door frames, making sure they don't overhang. Screw the panels to the frames with ¾"-long wood screws, keeping the frames square with the panels as you go. Finally, miter-cut 2" wainscot cap molding to fit around the edges of each door. Tape

the cap pieces to the door so they hold their position, then drill pilot holes through the pieces and the pegboard. Attach the cap frame to the doors with glue and 1" wire nails.

APPLY THE FINISHING TOUCHES. Fill all screw holes and exposed plywood edges with wood putty, and sand all rough edges and surfaces smooth. Apply glue to the tips of the pegs and insert them into the stretcher. Prime and paint the locker—we used enamel paint for a hard finish. Hang the doors with two 1½ × 2" butt hinges per door, then attach a pull or handle to each door. Install magnetic door catches for each door at the top and bottom of the divider.

TIP

Pegboard can be tricky to paint with a brush or roller—no matter how hard you try, the peg holes always seem to clog with paint, creating a ragged appearance. For best results, paint pegboard with spray paint or a paint sprayer.

Gardening Center

This combination worksurface and cabinet lets you centralize your gardening tools & supplies in one convenient location.

CONSTRUCTION MATERIALS

Quantity	Lumber
1	¼" × 4 × 4' hardboard
1	1 × 2" × 8' pine
2	¾" × 4 × 8' AC plywood
1	4"-dia. × 4' PVC drain pipe

This gardening center eliminates the spread of gardening supplies, while doing double duty as a functional gardening workstation. Positioned at a comfortable working height, the plywood worksurface lets you repot plants or blend soils without straining your back. The main cabinet is large enough to hold most of your fertilizers, seeds, and other supplies. A soil cart housed in the cabinet rolls out to make transporting heavy materials a snap. The tubes at the sides of the cabinet organize your long-handled gardening tools. And the high shelves at the top of the cabinet are perfect for storing pesticides and other products that should be kept out of the reach of children.

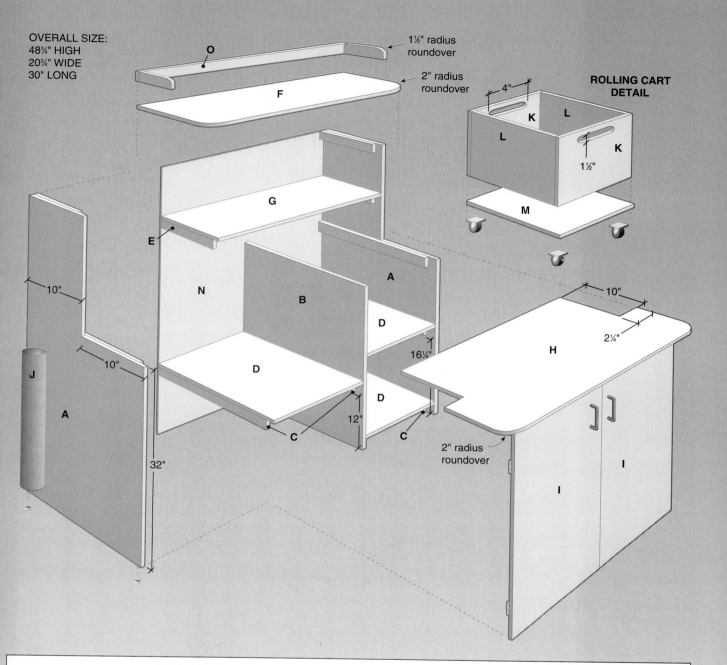

OVERALL SIZE:
48¾" HIGH
20¾" WIDE
30" LONG

1½" radius roundover

2" radius roundover

ROLLING CART DETAIL

4"

1½"

10"

10"

32"

16¼"

12"

10"

2¼"

2" radius roundover

Cutting List

Key	Part	Dimension	Pcs.	Material
A	Side panel	¾ × 20 × 48"	2	Plywood
B	Center partition	¾ × 20 × 32"	1	Plywood
C	Shelf cleat	¾ × 1½ × 18"	12	Plywood
D	Cabinet shelf	¾ × 13⅞ × 20"	3	Plywood
E	Shelf cleat	¾ × 1½ × 8"	4	Pine
F	Top shelf	¾ × 13 × 33"	1	Plywood
G	Middle shelf	¾ × 10 × 28½"	1	Plywood
H	Worksurface	¾ × 23 × 33"	1	Plywood

Cutting List

Key	Part	Dimension	Pcs.	Material
I	Door	¾ × 14¾ × 31⅞"	2	Plywood
J	Tool holder	4"-dia. × 24"	2	PVC
K	Box end	¾ × 12 × 10"	2	Plywood
L	Box side	¾ × 16 × 10"	2	Plywood
M	Box bottom	¾ × 12 × 17½"	1	Plywood
N	Back panel	¼ × 30 × 32¾"	1	Hardboard
O	Shelf skirt	¾ × 1½ × *	3	Pine

Materials: Wood glue, #6 × 1¼ wood screws, 4¼"-dia. × 1½" carriage bolts w/nuts and washers, glide feet (4), 2½"-dia. casters (4), self-closing cabinet hinges (4), door pulls (2), wood putty.

Note: Measurements reflect the actual size of dimensional lumber.
*Cut to fit

Cut along the straight cutting lines on the side panels with a circular saw, then use a jig saw or hand saw to finish the cuts at the corners.

Measure up from the bottom cabinet cleats to mark positions for the other cabinet shelf cleats.

Directions: Gardening Center

MAKE THE SIDE PANELS. The L-shaped plywood side panels for the gardening center support shelf cleats and the worksurface. Cut the sides (A) to size. Mark a point on one side edge of one plywood panel, 32" up from the bottom, to set the worksurface height. Draw a line perpendicular to the side edge at this point, then mark a point on the line 10" in from the edge. Mark another point 10" in from the top corner, at the same side, and connect the two 10" points to form the cutout area for the panel. Using a jig saw or circular saw, make the cutout. If you use a circular saw for the cutouts, you'll have to finish the corners of the cuts with a hand saw or a jig saw. Sand the edges smooth, then use the cut panel as a template to draw a matching cutout on the other side panel. Cut out the second side panel **(photo A).**

INSTALL THE SHELF CLEATS. The cabinet shelves are supported by 1 × 2 cleats mounted on the inside faces of the cabinet sides and on a center divider panel. Cut the divider (B) to size from ¾"-thick plywood. Then, cut the cabinet cleats (C) and shelf cleats (E) to size from 1 × 2 pine. Sand the plywood surfaces and edges with medium-grit sandpaper and a power sander. Attach a cleat to the inside face of each side panel, flush with the bottom and the back edge (the 2" setback between the cleats and the front edges of the panels is to conceal the front end of the cleat). Use wood glue and #6 × 1¼" wood screws to attach the cleats. Also attach a cleat on each side of the divider, flush with the bottom and back. Mark points 16¼" up from the bottom at the front and back edges of the right side panel and on one side of the divider **(photo B).** Also mark points 12½" up from the bottom edge of the left side panel, and on the unmarked face of the divider. Draw lines connecting the points on the inside faces of the sides and on both faces of the divider. Attach cleats just below the lines, flush with the back edges of the sides and the divider. On the side panels, attach cleats so the top edges are flush with the bottoms of the cutouts, and the ends are flush with the back ends of the panels. Mark lines for the lower shelf cleats in the area above the worksurface, 9" above the tops of the cleats at the worksurface cutout. Attach the shelf cleats (E) just below the lines, flush with the back edges of the sides. Also attach cleats flush with the tops of the side panels to help support the upper shelf.

INSTALL THE SHELVES. Cut the cabinet shelves (D) and middle shelf (G) to size. Prop the side panels in an upright position, about 33" apart, with their cleated surfaces facing in. Attach the lower shelf in the area above the worksurface, using glue and #6 × 1¼" wood screws—counterbore pilot

The cabinet shelves and upper shelves are attached to the sides and the divider to give the gardening center side-to-side strength.

holes for the screws so the heads can be covered with wood putty. Prop the divider up between the sides, making sure the cleats are lined up correctly with the matching cleats on the side panels. Attach the cabinet shelves, making sure the front and back edges are flush with the edges of the side panels **(photo C).**

MAKE THE TOP SHELF. Cut the top shelf (F) to size from plywood. Draw cutting lines for roundovers on the front corners of the shelf, using a compass set for a 2" radius. Cut the roundovers with a jig saw. Use a power sander to smooth out the cuts. For decorative appeal and to prevent items from slipping off the top shelf, we added skirt boards (O) to the back and ends of the shelf. First, cut a 1 × 2 to the same length as the shelf. Next, cut two pieces of 1 × 2 to 4" in length. Draw a 1½"-radius roundover at one end of each piece (see *Diagram,* page 13). Cut the roundovers and sand smooth. Attach the back skirt board to

the back of the shelf, on edge and flush at the ends. Use glue and #6 × 1¼" wood screws driven up through the shelf and into the skirt board. Fasten the side skirts to the ends of the shelf, with the square end of each piece butted up against the back skirt board **(photo D).** Fasten the top shelf to the top cleats on the side panels.

BUILD & ATTACH THE WORK-SURFACE. The worksurface is notched to fit around the top shelf sections of the side panels. Rounded over at the front corners, it overhangs the lower sections of the side panels on the front and sides. Cut the worksurface (H) to size from ¾"-thick plywood. Mark 10"-deep × 2¼"-wide notches at the back corners to fit around the sides (see *Diagram,* page 13). Use a compass set for a 2" radius to mark roundover cutting lines at the front corners of the worksurface. Make the cutouts with a jig saw, then smooth out with a sander **(photo E).** Test-

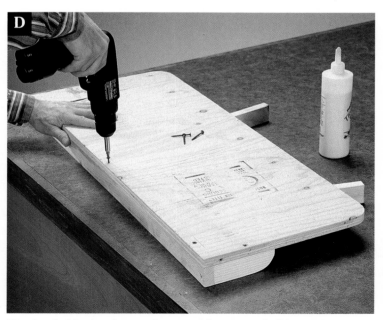

The 1 × 2 skirt that frames the top of the upper shelf keeps items from falling off. Screw the skirt pieces in from below.

Use a jig saw to cut notches into the sides of the worksurface so it fits around the side panels.

Insert a pen or pencil into the guide holes in each side panel and mark drilling points on the pipes.

fit the worksurface, checking to make sure the cabinet assembly is square at the same time. Set the worksurface onto the horizontal arms of the side-panel cutouts, with the notches fitting around the sides and the overhang equal from side to side. Attach the worksurface to the cleats with glue and screws.

MAKE & ATTACH THE TOOL HOLDERS. We mounted 2'-long sections of PVC drainpipe to the outside faces of the side panels to create holders for long-handled garden tools. Cut a section of 4"-dia. PVC drainpipe into two 24" lengths to make the tool holders (J). A hacksaw is a good tool choice for cutting PVC. Smooth out the cuts with emery paper or very fine sandpaper. If you plan to paint the PVC tool holders, buff the pipes with medium-grit sandpaper to create a better bonding surface for the paint (this activity is called scarifying). Draw reference lines for hanging the tool hold-

ers on the outer faces of the side panels. The lines should be parallel to the back edges, 7" in. On the reference lines, mark drilling points 4" and 24" up from the bottom edges of the side panels. Drill ¼"-dia. guide holes for carriage bolts at these points. Mark matching guide holes on the tool holders by positioning the pipes on the centerlines so the holes in the side panels fall 2" in from the top and bottom of each pipe. Insert a pen into the guide holes, from the inside, and mark the hole locations onto the surface of the pipes **(photo F).** Drill ¼"-dia. holes at these points. Place the pipes in position, with the guide holes aligned, and insert carriage bolts from inside each pipe, threaded through so the ends project out past the inside faces of the side panels. Attach washers and nuts to the ends of the carriage bolts and tighten securely—do not overtighten.

ATTACH THE BACK PANEL. Cut the back panel (N) to size from ¼" hardboard using a circular saw. Position the back panel at the back of the cabinet assembly, and attach it with 2d common (box) nails. Keep the edges of the back panel flush with the outside surfaces of the side panels and the top of the worksurface. If the cabinet appears to be out of square, check it by measuring the diagonal measurements across the back to make sure they are the same. Do not attach the back panel until you are certain the cabinet is square (one of the main jobs of the back panel is to keep the cabinet from slipping out of square).

ATTACH THE DOORS. Cut the cabinet doors (I) to size from ¾"-thick plywood. Attach hinges (we used self-closing cabinet door hinges sized for ¾"-thick wood) to the outside, back faces of the doors **(photo G).** The hinges should be positioned 2" down from the top edge of each door, and 4" up

Hang the cabinet doors with self-closing cabinet hinges to keep the doors from swinging open.

from the bottoms. Position the doors over the front of the cabinet, with a ⅛" gap between doors. Mark the hinge screw locations onto the inside faces of the side panels, then remove the doors and drill pilot holes at the screw locations. Hang the doors.

MAKE THE SOIL CART. The rolling soil cart lets you transport blended potting soils from the work area to the garden without creating back strain. Start by cutting the box sides (L), box ends (K) and box bottom (M) to size from ¾" plywood. Mark hand-grip cutouts on the box ends: the bottom of each cutout should be 3½" down from the top edge of the box end; the top should be 2" down; the ends of the cutouts should be 4" in from the side edges. Draw roundovers at the ends of the cutouts, then make the handgrip cutouts with a jig saw (you'll need to drill a starter hole inside the cutout line first). Sand the edges

smooth. Attach the box ends to the box sides with glue and screws driven to form butt joints (see *Diagram,* page 13). Check to make sure the four-piece frame is square when assembled, then attach the box bottom to the sides and ends.

Attach casters to the underside of the box bottom **(photo H).** The casters (we used 2½"-dia. casters) should be positioned an inch or two inside each corner. If the screws that come with the casters are more than ¾" in length, substitute shorter screws with the same shank size.

APPLY FINISHING TOUCHES. Attach nail-on glide feet to the bottom edges of the side panels to minimize ground contact. Fill all screw counterbores with wood putty, sand smooth, then finish-sand all wood surfaces. Apply a finish (we used green exterior paint). You may wish to remove the door before applying the finish. Also paint the tool holders, if you wish. Once the finish is dry, attach door pulls to the doors—we used 3" plastic pulls mounted about 3" down from the top of each door.

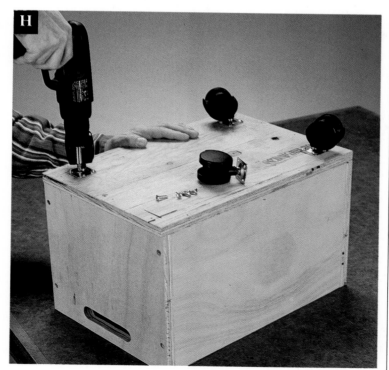

Fasten the casters to the bottom corners of the soil cart, using screws that are no more than ¾" long.

PROJECT
POWER TOOLS

Entry Valet

The friendly face of this valet hides the fact that it's a functional storage unit, with a drop-down bin and a covered scarf box.

CONSTRUCTION MATERIALS

Quantity	Lumber
1	1 × 10" × 6' pine
1	1 × 12" × 6' pine
1	1 × 6" × 6' pine
1	1 × 4" × 6' pine
1	1 × 3" × 6' pine
1	¾" × 6' pine stop molding
1	¼" × 4 × 4' plywood

This entry valet is designed to provide handy storage in one of the busiest areas of your house—the entryway. It is equipped with a spacious pivoting bin at the top, and a scarf storage box with a hinged lid that also functions as a shelf and a stretcher to give the valet added strength.

Because the entry is the first part of your house that most visitors will see, it is important that entry furnishings be pleasing to look at, as well as functional. For that reason, we used simple construction that is reminiscent of popular Shaker styling, and added decorative contours that give the valet a touch of Colonial style as well.

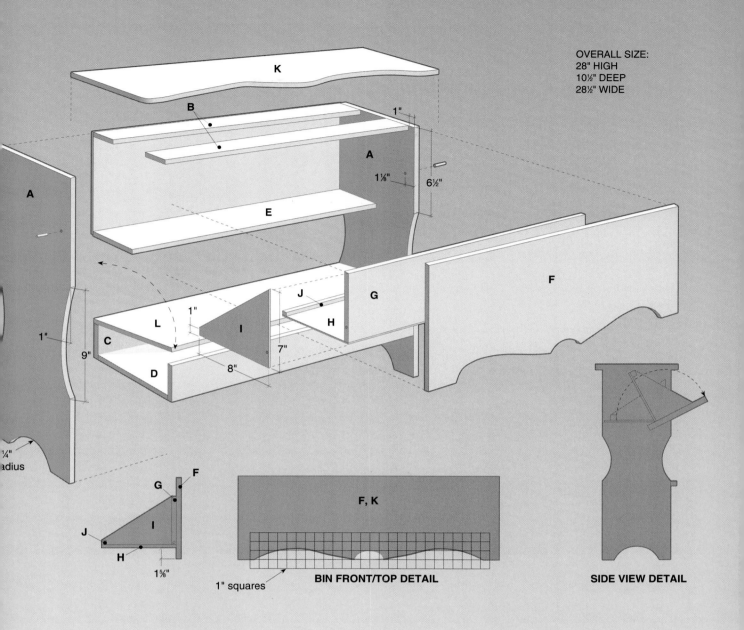

BIN FRONT/TOP DETAIL

1" squares

F, K

SIDE VIEW DETAIL

Cutting List

Key	Part	Dimension	Pcs.	Material
A	End	¾ × 9¼ × 33¼"	2	Pine
B	Top stretcher	¾ × 2½ × 28½"	2	Pine
C	Box side	¾ × 3½ × 28½"	2	Pine
D	Box bottom	¾ × 7¾ × 28½"	1	Pine
E	Bin stop	¾ × 5½ × 28½"	1	Pine
F	False front	¾ × 9¼ × 28¼"	1	Pine
G	Bin front	¾ × 5½ × 27⅝"	1	Pine

Cutting List

Key	Part	Dimension	Pcs.	Material
H	Bin bottom	¼ × 8 × 27⅝"	1	Plywood
I	Bin side	¾ × 7 × 8"	2	Plywood
J	Bin back lip	¾ × ¾ × 27⅝"	1	Stop molding
K	Top	¾ × 10¼ × 32"	1	Pine
L	Lid	¾ × 9½ × 28¼"	1	Pine
M	Valet back	¾ × 8 × 29½"	1	Plywood

Materials: Wood glue, 1" wire nails, #6 × 1¼" wood screw, finishing materials, 2" butt hinges (2).

Note: Measurements reflect the actual size of dimensional lumber.

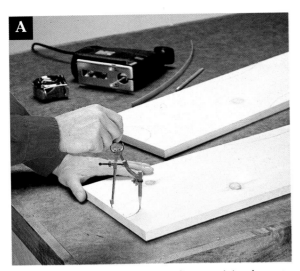

Use a compass to draw 2¼"-radius semicircular cutting lines on the bottoms of the end pieces.

Fasten the bin stop board between the end panels to complete the assembly of the basic valet framework.

Fasten the bin sides with wire nails and glue.

Directions: Entry Valet

CUT & CONTOUR THE END PIECES. The ends of the valet are made from pieces of 1 × 10 pine with curved contours cut at the sides and at the bottom of each panel. Cut the end panels (A) to size. To make the side cutouts, mark points at each side edge, 17⅜" from the bottom of each end. At the points, measure in 1" from the edge to mark the deepest point of each side cutout. Mark points 4½" above and below each mark at the side edges to mark the endpoints for the cutouts. Draw smooth, curved lines from endpoint to endpoint, through the centerpoints. To draw the lines, flex a ruler between endpoints as a guide, or make a cardboard template to trace the cutouts. Make the cutouts with a jig saw, then sand out any rough spots. To make the bottom cutouts, mark the center of each end panel on the bottom edge. Set a compass to 2¼" radius, and set the tip on a centerpoint. Draw a semicircular cutting line at the bottom of each panel (photo A). Make the cutouts and sand smooth.

ASSEMBLE THE FRAMEWORK. The contoured end pieces are fitted together with the scarf box (C, D), the top stretchers (B), and the bin stop (E) to make the general framework for the valet. Cut these pieces to size. Build the scarf box by fastening together the bottom and the sides with glue and #6 × 1¼" screws. Counterbore pilot holes to accept ⅜"-dia. wood plugs. Three or four evenly spaced screws driven through the box sides and into the edges of the box bottom are plenty. Attach the box assembly to the inside faces of the end panels, so the box sides are flush with the front and back edges of the end panels. The bottom of the box should be 7¼" up from the bottoms of the end panels. Attach the top stretchers between the end panels, flat face up, using glue and counterbored screws. One stretcher should be flush with the back and top edges of the end panels, and the other should be flush with the tops, but recessed 1" from the front edges (see *Diagram*, page 19). Finally, install the bin stop between the end panels, 7½" down from the tops of the panels, and flush with the back edges (photo B).

BUILD THE BIN. The dropdown bin pivots on dowels to open up for storage. Cut the bin front (G) and the bin bottom (H). Attach the bin bottom to the bin front with glue and 1" wire nails driven up through the bottom and into the front piece. Next, cut the triangular bin sides (I) (see *Diagram*, page 19). Attach the sides to the bottom/front assembly with

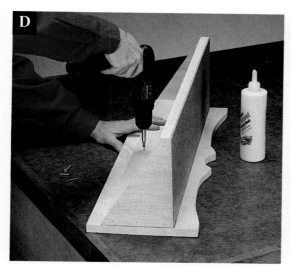

Drive wood screws through the inside of the bin and into the back of the false front.

Clamp the bin to the valet framework, then drill dowel holes through the sides and into the bin.

glue and wire nails **(photo C)**. Cut a piece of ¾ × ¾" pine stop molding to length to make the bin back lip (J). Glue the lip to the bin bottom so the ends fit between the bin sides.

MAKE & ATTACH THE FALSE FRONT FOR THE BIN. The false front (F) is attached to the front of the bin to create a decorative apron for the valet. To make the false front, cut a piece of 1 × 10 pine to size, then plot out a grid with 1" squares on the face of the board. Using the pattern on page 19 as a guide, draw the cutout shape onto the false front, and cut out with a jig saw. Sand smooth. Draw a reference line on the inside face of the false front, 1⅝" up from the bottom edge. Attach the false front to the bin front so the bin rides on the reference line. Use glue and #6 × 1¼" wood screws driven through the bin, and into the false front **(photo D).**

INSTALL THE BIN. Set the completed bin onto the bin stop board between the end panels so it is flush against the outside top stretcher and the bin stop.

Use spacer blocks and C-clamps to hold the bin in place. Mount a portable drill stand to your portable drill, and drill a ⅜"-dia. × 1⅝"-deep hole through each end panel and into the sides of the bin **(photo E)**. The center-points of the holes should be 6½" down from the tops of the end panels, and 1⅛" in from the front edges. Cut two 1½"-long pieces from a ⅜"-dia. dowel, and insert them in the holes. Remove the C-clamps.

APPLY THE FINISHING TOUCHES. With the bin still pinned in place, cut the valet top (K) to size, then make the decorative cutout on the front edge using the same pattern and techniques used for the bin false front (the valet top does not have the small scallop in the center that is cut into the false front). Also cut the scarf box lid (L). Remove the bin, finish-sand all surfaces, and apply your finish of choice. We used orange shellac (a traditional finishing product for pine). Once the parts are finished, attach the lid to the box with 2" butt hinges at the back of the lid, and attach the valet

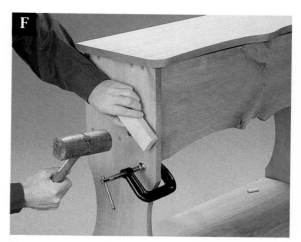

Using a wood block to prevent splitting, drive dowels into the dowel holes to serve as pivots.

top to the end panels with glue and wood screws counter-bored for wood plugs. Before installing the bin, squirt wood glue into the dowel holes in the bin. Replace the bin, and drive the dowels into the dowel holes. Use a wood block to prevent splitting the dowels **(photo F).** After the glue sets, sand the dowels flush with the sides of the valet, and stain to match the rest of the wood. Cut a back (M) for the valet and tack it to the back edges of the end panels and to the top stretcher, using wire nails.

Pet Supply Center

Store pet equipment, medicine and food in this all-in-one storage center with a built-in pet food dispenser.

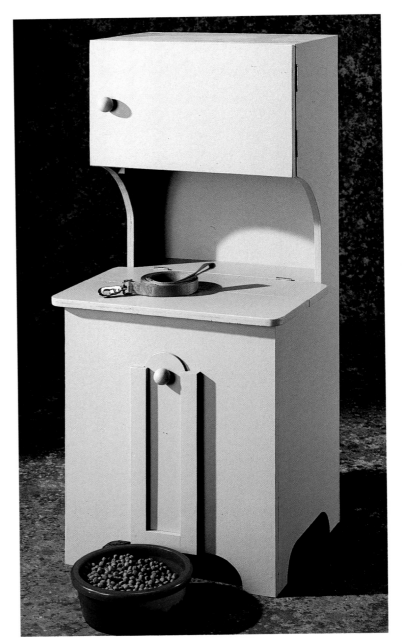

Most pet owners know that keeping track of all of the necessary equipment and supplies your pet needs can sometimes get a little overwhelming. With this uniquely designed pet supply center, you can keep all the necessary items for your pet in one central unit. In addition, this storage center has a built-in pet food bin and dispenser to eliminate wrestling with bulky and messy pet food bags and scoops every time your pet's dinner bell rings. Simply place the pet's dish below the dispenser opening and raise the hopper until the bowl is full.

The bi-fold lid can be used as a countertop, but it also flips up easily to make loading pet food into the bin easy. The upper cabinet is a suitable place for just about any pet things you need to store, such as cans of pet food, medicine, grooming equipment, pet food and water dishes, or leashes and collars. Built mostly from plywood, the pet supply center can be finished so it fits into just about any area of your house.

CONSTRUCTION MATERIALS

Quantity	Lumber
1	¼" × 2 × 4' hardboard
1	⅜" × 2 × 4' AC plywood
1	¾" × 4 × 8' AC plywood
1	1 × 2" × 10' pine

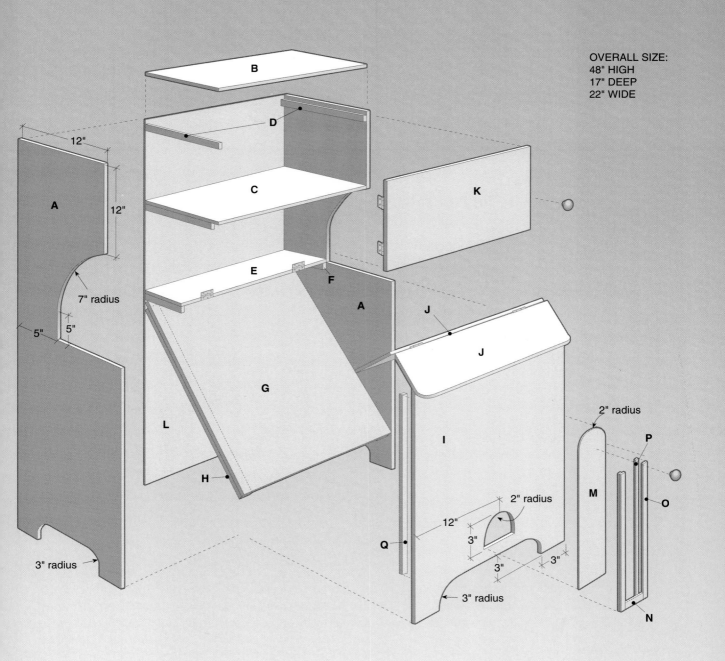

OVERALL SIZE:
48" HIGH
17" DEEP
22" WIDE

Cutting List

Key	Part	Dimension	Pcs.	Material
A	Side panel	¾ × 17 × 48"	2	Plywood
B	Top panel	¾ × 12 × 18½"	1	Plywood
C	Cabinet shelf	¾ × 12 × 18½"	1	Plywood
D	Cabinet cleat	¾ × 1½ × 12"	4	Pine
E	Lid support	¾ × 5 × 18½"	1	Plywood
F	Lid cleat	¾ × 1½ × 17"	2	Pine
G	Bin tray	¾ × 18½ × 24"	1	Plywood
H	Bin tray cleat	¾ × 1½ × 21"	2	Pine
I	Front panel	¾ × 20 × 24"	1	Plywood

Cutting List

Key	Part	Dimension	Pcs.	Material
J	Lid half	¾ × 22 × 7"	2	Plywood
K	Cabinet door	¼ × 12 × 20"	1	Plywood
L	Back panel	¼ × 20 × 48"	1	Hardboard
M	Hopper door	¼ × 4 × 16"	1	Hardboard
N	Door stop	⅜ × 1½ × 13½"	1	Pine
O	Door track (front)	¾ × 1¼ × 12"	2	Plywood
P	Door track (back)	¾ × 1 × 12"	2	Plywood
Q	Corner cleat	¾ × 1½ × 18"	2	Pine

Materials: Wood glue, #6 × 1¼" wood screws, 2d common nails, (6) 2 × 2" butt hinges, drawer knob, finishing materials.

Note: Measurements reflect the actual size of dimensional lumber.

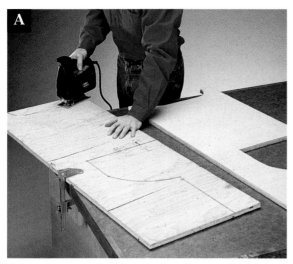

Make the curved cutouts in the side panels using a jig saw.

Mark the cleat positions on the side panel, using a framing square to make sure the lines are perpendicular to the sides of the panels.

Directions:
Pet Supply Center

MAKE THE SIDE PANELS. Start by cutting the side panels (A) to size from ¾" plywood, using a circular saw and straightedge cutting guide. Draw cutting lines onto one side panel for the flat-topped arc that is cut in the bottom to create the feet, and for the quarter-round recess that is cut out level with the top of the food bin. The *Diagram* on page 23 contains all the cutting information you'll need to plot and cut these shapes. Use a jig saw to cut out the bottom arc and the lid recess. Sand both cutouts smooth, then use the side panel as a template to mark the other side panel. Cut and sand the second panel **(photo A).**

MAKE & ATTACH THE CLEATS. The shelves in the cabinet area, the bi-fold lid and lid support, and the tray in the food bin are supported by cleats mounted on the inside faces of the side panels. Cleats also are used at the joints between the front panel and the side panels. Cut the cabinet cleats (D), the lid

Fasten the shelf cleats and tray cleats to the side panels at their marked positions using wood glue and screws.

cleats (F), the bin tray cleats (H) and the corner cleats (Q) from 1 × 2 pine. Mark the tops and bottoms of the lid cleats so they are flush with the straight bottoms of the recess cutouts (see *Diagram,* page 23). To lay out the locations for the bin tray cleats, draw a diagonal line on each side panel, starting 3¾" up from the bottom at the front edge, and running to the bottom of the lid cleat location, where it meets the back edge of the side panel. This line marks the position for the bottom of the ¾"-thick bin tray.

Draw a second diagonal line on each panel, parallel to the first and 1½" below it to mark the bottom edge of the bin tray cleat on each panel. Lay out the top and bottom locations for the cabinet cleats on the inside surfaces of the side panels **(photo B).** One pair of cleats should be flush with the tops of the panels, and the bottoms of the other pair should be 12" down from the tops of the panels. Use a framing square to make sure these lines are perpendicular to the sides of the panels. Attach cleats at the

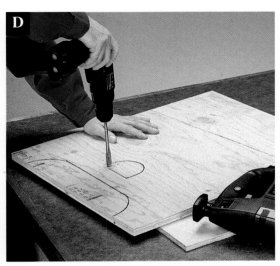

Drill a starter hole, then cut the dispenser opening with a jig saw.

lines with glue and #6 × 1¼" wood screws **(photo C).** You may need to trim the ends of the lower cabinet cleats or the bin tray cleats so they do not stick out past the edges of the side panels. Finally, attach the corner cleats flush with the front edges of the side panels, centered between the bin tray cleats and the lid cleats.

ATTACH THE TOP, SHELF, LID SUPPORT & TRAY. Cut the top (B), cabinet shelf (C), lid support (E), and bin tray (G). Sand the surfaces and edges of all pieces with medium-grit sandpaper and a power sander. Prop the side panels up with the inside faces facing one another. Glue and screw the top, cabinet shelf, lid supports and tray to the appropriate cleats on the side panels. Make sure the front and back edges of the parts are flush with the front and back edges of the side panels.

MAKE & ATTACH THE FRONT PANEL. Cut the front panel (I) to size from ¾"-thick plywood. Draw cutout shapes for the flat-topped arc at the bottom of the panel, and the bin dispenser hole, according to the dimensions in the *Diagram* on page 23. Drill a starter hole inside the dispenser hole cutout **(photo D),** then make both cutouts with a jig saw and sand the edges smooth. Attach the front panel to the corner cleats at the front edges of the side panels.

ATTACH THE LID & CABINET DOOR. The lid for the bin is made of two pieces of plywood hinged together so they open like a bi-fold door. Cut the lid halves (J) and the cabinet door (K). Use a jig saw to round over the front corners of the front half of the lid to about a 1" radius. Press the square edge of the front half against an edge of the back half of the lid, and join them together with two 2 × 2" butt hinges mounted on the undersides of the lid halves. Mount the lid assembly to the lid support with two 2 × 2" butt hinges **(photo E).** Attach the cabinet door to the side panel with two 2 × 2" butt hinges.

INSTALL THE HOPPER DOOR. The hopper door slides up and down over the dispenser hole to let pet food flow out of the bin. Cut the hopper door (M), the door stop (N), and the front and back door tracks (O, P). Use a compass set to a 2" radius to draw a roundover cutting line at the top of the hopper door, and cut the roundover with a jig saw. Attach a drawer knob to the hopper door. The door is fitted inside tracks so it can slide up and down. Attach the door stop to the front panel with glue and screws, directly below the dispenser opening and flush with the top edge of the arc cutout on the front panel. Attach the back door tracks to the front panel in a vertical position, ¼" away from each end of the stop and flush with the arc cutout. Tack the front door tracks on top of the back tracks so their outside edges are flush. Insert the hopper door inside the tracks.

APPLY FINISHING TOUCHES. Cut the back panel (L) and fasten it to the back of the unit with 2d common nails. Fill screw counterbores and exposed plywood edges with wood putty, then sand all surfaces smooth. Apply your finish of choice (we used enamel paint).

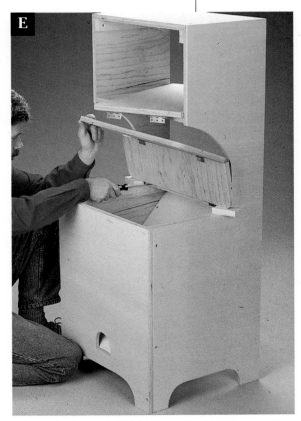

Mount the hinged, bi-fold lid to the lid support with butt hinges.

STORE IT IN STYLE 25

Pine Pantry

*Turn a remote corner or closet into a kitchen pantry
with this charming pine cabinet.*

CONSTRUCTION MATERIALS

Quantity	Lumber
3	1 × 10" × 8' pine
4	1 × 8" × 8' pine
1	1 × 6" × 8' pine
1	1 × 4" × 8' pine
5	1 × 3" × 8' pine
2	1 × 2" × 10' pine
1	¾" × 4 × 8' plywood
1	¼" × 4 × 8' plywood

This compact pantry cabinet is absolutely ideal for keeping your kitchen organized and efficient. It features a convenient turntable shelf, or "Lazy Susan," on the inside of the cabinet for easy access to canned foods. A swing-out shelf assembly on the opposite side lets you get the most from the pantry's space. Its roominess allows you to store almost all your non-refrigerated food items.

But the best feature of the pantry is its appearance. The rugged beauty of the cabinet hides its simplicity. For such an impressive-looking project, it is remarkably easy to make, so even if you don't have a traditional pantry in your home, you can have a convenient, attractive storage center.

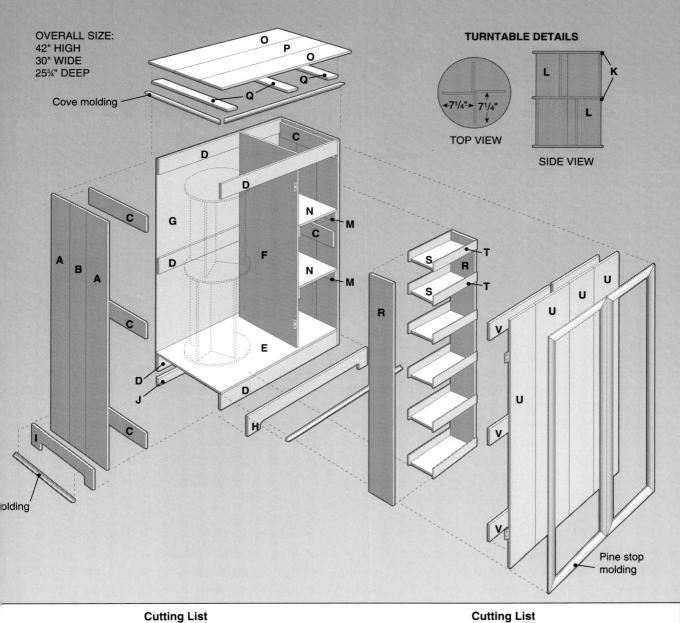

OVERALL SIZE:
42" HIGH
30" WIDE
25¾" DEEP

Cove molding

TURNTABLE DETAILS

TOP VIEW

SIDE VIEW

Pine stop molding

Cutting List

Key	Part	Dimension	Pcs.	Material
A	Side board	¾ × 9¼ × 39¼"	4	Pine
B	Middle board	¾ × 5½ × 39¼"	2	Pine
C	Panel cleat	¾ × 2½ × 22½"	6	Pine
D	Stretcher	¾ × 2½ × 26½"	5	Pine
E	Floor	¾ × 24 × 26½"	1	Plywood
F	Divider	¾ × 22½ × 36"	1	Plywood
G	Back	¼ × 28 × 39¼"	1	Plywood
H	Base front	¾ × 3½ × 29½"	1	Pine
I	Base side	¾ × 3½ × 24¼"	2	Pine
J	Base back	¾ × 1½ × 28"	1	Pine
K	Turntable shelf	¾ × 16"-dia.	3	Plywood

Cutting List

Key	Part	Dimension	Pcs.	Material
L	Supports	¾ × 17¼ × 12"	8	Pine
M	Shelf cleat	¾ × 1½ × 22"	4	Pine
N	Fixed shelf	¾ × 9 × 23"	2	Plywood
O	Top board	¾ × 9½ × 30"	2	Pine
P	Middle board	¾ × 7¼ × 30"	1	Pine
Q	Top cleat	¾ × 2½ × 22"	3	Pine
R	Swing-out end	¾ × 6 × 32"	2	Pine
S	Swing-out shelf	¾ × 6 × 10"	6	Pine
T	Swing-out side	¾ × 2 × 11½"	12	Plywood
U	Door board	¾ × 6⅝ × 35"	4	Plywood
V	Door cleat	¾ × 2½ × 11"	6	Plywood

Materials: Glue, ¾" cove molding, ⅜ × 1¼" stop molding, wood screws (#6 × 1¼"), 1" wire nails, 2d finish nails, turntable hardware, cabinet handles, brass hinges (3 × 3"), finishing materials.

Note: Measurements reflect the actual size of dimensional lumber.

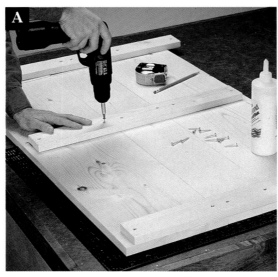
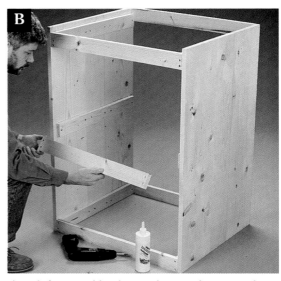

Use cleats to fasten side and middle boards, forming the cabinet sides.

Attach front and back stretchers at the top and bottom, and a middle stretcher at the back.

Directions: Pine Pantry

MAKE THE CABINET SIDES. Each cabinet side is made from three pine boards fastened together with three 1 × 3 cleats. Start by cutting the side boards (A), middle boards (B) and panel cleats (C) to size. Sand all parts with medium-grit sandpaper to smooth out any rough edges after cutting. Position a middle board between two side boards, making sure all top and bottom edges are flush. As you assemble the sides, butt the boards against a framing square to keep them in line. Position a panel cleat widthwise across the boards so the bottom edge of the cleat is flush with the bottom edges of the boards. The ends of the cleat should be ¾" from the outside edges of the side boards. Fasten the cleat to the boards with glue and #6 × 1¼" wood screws. Attach the next panel cleat to the boards so its top edge is 21½" up from the bottom edge of the first cleat

(photo A). Maintain a ¾" distance from the cleat ends to the board edges. Install the top panel cleat with its top edge 1" down from the board tops. Repeat these steps to make the other cabinet side.

ATTACH THE SIDES. Connect the two sides by attaching side stretchers (D) between them. Attach the stretchers by driving screws through them into the ends of the panel cleats. Start by cutting the stretchers to length. Attach them at the front and back of the cabinet along the bottom, making sure their top and bottom edges are flush with the top and bottom edges of the panel cleats. The top two stretchers are positioned a little differently—while the back stretcher is flush with the tops and bottoms of the panel cleats, the front stretcher is positioned flush with the top edges of the cabinet sides. Finally, attach one stretcher at the back of the cabinet, flush with the panel cleats on the middle of the cabinet sides **(photo B).**

ATTACH THE FLOOR. The floor (E) of the pantry organizer is attached to the tops of the bottom stretchers and panel cleats. Start by cutting the floor to size from ¾"-thick plywood. Fill any voids in the front and back edges of the floor with wood putty. Glue the parts and fasten the floor between the cabinet sides by driving wood screws through the floor into the stretchers and panel cleats.

ATTACH THE DIVIDER. The divider fits inside the cabinet, and has shelf cleats attached to it to hold the cabinet shelves in place. Begin by cutting the divider (F) and shelf cleats (M) to size. Draw a line across the floor, 9" from the right-hand cabinet side—this line marks the position of the divider's outside face. Measure and mark shelf cleat position lines on the right-hand cabinet side 10" and 20¾" up from the cabinet floor. Draw corresponding lines on the divider. These lines mark the top edges of the shelf cleats. Use glue and wood screws to fasten the shelf cleats

Install the divider 9" in from the right-hand side of the cabinet.

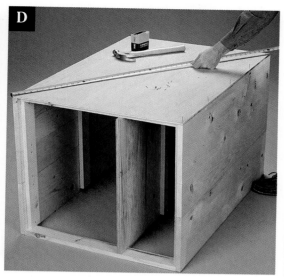

Check for square by measuring diagonally between the corners to make sure the distances are equal.

to the divider and side with their top edges at the lines. Insert the divider into the cabinet with its cleated face facing the cleated cabinet side. Apply glue to the bottom edge of the divider. Drive wood screws up through the cabinet floor into the bottom divider edge, and drive 4d finish nails through the top stretchers and into the divider edge **(photo C).**

ATTACH THE BACK. The back (G) is made from ¼"-thick plywood and is tacked to the cabinet side edges and stretchers with 1" wire nails. Cut the back to size, and drive evenly spaced nails into one side edge. Measure diagonally across the opposite corners on the back to check if the cabinet is square **(photo D).** If the two diagonal measurements are different, your cabinet isn't square. Square up the cabinet, if needed, by applying pressure to the opposite corners. Drive evenly spaced nails into the stretchers and edges to secure the back to the cabinet.

ATTACH THE FIXED SHELVES. The fixed shelves (N) fit between the divider and cabinet side. They are fastened permanently to help keep the cabinet square. Cut the fixed shelves to size from ¾"-thick plywood, and attach them to the cleats with glue and wood screws.

MAKE THE BASE. The base is made of four pine boards that are scooped out on their bottom edges to create a foot at each corner. Start by cutting the base front (H), base sides (I), and base back (J) to size. Sand the parts, then use a compass to draw 1"-radius semicircles, 5½" from each end of the base front, centered top to bottom. Using a straight-edge, draw a straight line connecting the tops of the circles. Repeat these steps on the

base sides, only center the semicircles 4¾" from the front and 5½" from the back. Cut along the lines with a jig saw. Mark lines ½" from the bottom edge on the rear edges of the base sides. These lines mark the position of the bottom edge of the base back. Glue the parts, then attach the base sides to the base front by driving 4d finish nails through the base front into the base side edges. Attach the base back between the base sides along

Cut the round turntable shelves with a jig saw. Each turntable shelf has an 8" radius.

Assemble the turntable supports in three pairs, joined at right angles.

Using 4d finish nails, attach the swing-out shelf side.

the marked lines. The bottom edge of the base back should be ½" from the bottom edges of the base sides. Set the nails.

ATTACH THE CABINET & BASE. With the cabinet on its back, slide the base over its bottom edges until the base back is flush with the bottom cleats. The base should extend 2" below the pantry's bottom edges. Drive counterbored #6 × 2" wood screws through the pantry sides into the base sides, and #6 × 1¼" wood screws through the front stretchers into the base front.

BUILD THE TURNTABLE SHELVES. The turntable shelves are made by cutting three circular plywood parts from square stock. They are attached to each other with pine supports. Once these parts are assembled they are mounted on a turntable, or "Lazy Susan." Start by cutting the turntable shelves (K) and turntable supports (L) to size. To cut the turntable shelves into their final, circular shape, mark the center of the turntable shelves, and use a compass to draw the turntable shelves' guidelines.

Each shelf should have an 8" radius. Cut the shelves to size with a jig saw **(photo E).** Attach pairs of turntable supports at right angles by applying glue and driving counterbored screws through one support's face into the other support's edge **(photo F),** forming simple butt joints. To attach the turntable supports to the turntable shelves (see *Diagram*, page 27), use a straightedge to scribe a line on the shelves, directly through their centerpoints. Place one pair of supports along the line with the joint at the centerpoint. Make sure the support pair forms a right angle, then outline the supports on the shelf. Position another support pair on the other side of the line and draw the outline. Drill pilot holes for #6 × 1¼" wood screws centered within the outlines, and fasten the turntable shelves to the turntable supports with glue and wood screws. The supports should have their spines meeting at the centerpoint of the turntable. Attach the turntable hardware to the bottom face of

the bottom turntable shelf, following manufacturer's directions. It is critical to center the turntable on the shelf, or the assembly will not rotate smoothly. Insert the turntable assembly after you apply the finish to the pantry organizer.

BUILD THE SWING-OUT RACK. Six swing-out shelves are attached between two shelf ends to make the rack. When completed, the rack swings on hinges to give you easy access to cans or dry goods. Cut the swing-out shelves (S), swing-out ends (R) and swing-out sides (T). Starting from one end, mark lines 6" apart up the swing-out ends. These lines mark the positions of the swing-out shelves. Apply glue to the shelf edges, then attach them to the swing-out ends by driving wood screws through the ends into the shelf edges. The bottom shelf should be flush with the bottom of the end edges. Finally, attach the swing-out shelf sides (T) on the edges of the shelves with glue and 1" wire nails **(photo G).** Set the swing-out rack aside until you have applied the finish.

Use a circular saw with a straightedge guide to rip-cut the door boards to size.

Tack pine cove molding frame around the edges of the assembled doors.

MAKE THE TOP. Cut the top boards (O), middle board (P) and top cleats (Q) to size. Sand them, and join the top boards and middle board by attaching a top cleat across the inside faces of the boards, 1¾" from each end. Fasten the third top cleat so its right-hand edge is 11½" from the right-hand edge of the top. When the top is placed on the cabinet, the right edge of this middle cleat should touch the divider. Position the top onto the cabinet, and fasten it by driving 4d finish nails into the cabinet sides and through the divider, into the middle cleat.

BUILD THE DOORS. Each door is made from two boards, held together with three cleats. The outside faces of the doors are framed with stop molding. Cut the door boards (U) and door cleats (V) to size **(photo H).** Use glue and counterbored wood screws to attach the top and bottom door cleats; the top edges of the top cleats should be 2" down from the tops of the boards. The bottom edges of the bottom cleats should be 3½" up from the bottoms of the boards. Center and attach the final door cleat on the inside faces of the door panels. Miter-cut ⅜"-thick stop molding to frame the front faces of the doors. Fasten the molding with glue and 1" wire nails **(photo I).**

APPLY FINISHING TOUCHES. Miter-cut ¾"-thick cove molding to fit around the base and top (see *Diagram*, page 27). Attach the molding with 2d finish nails and glue. Fill all nail holes, and finish-sand the pantry organizer with fine (150- or 180-grit) sandpaper. We applied a clear polyurethane finish to the outside and inside surfaces. Attach two evenly spaced 3 × 3" butt hinges to the edges of the swing-out rack, and mount it on the divider **(photo J).** Position ¼"-thick spacers between the rack and divider to create a clearance for the shelf to swing. Attach the turntable assembly to the floor of the pantry organizer—check to make sure the turntable rotates freely. Attach hinges and handles to the doors, then mount the doors to the cabinet sides.

With ¼"-thick spacers in place beneath the swing-out rack, attach the rack to the divider with 3 × 3" butt hinges.

PROJECT
POWER TOOLS

Recipe Box

*This cozy home for your favorite recipe cards
will fit into just about any kitchen decor.*

With this simple recipe box, you can store recipe cards with a straightforward style that never goes out of fashion. Made from ½"-thick aspen boards, this de-sign features just enough inter-esting shapes and contours to give it a distinctive appearance, without becoming so ornamen-tal that it is excluded from many popular decorating schemes.

Most recipe boxes are built to hold standard 3 × 5 index cards. But if, like most people, not all of your recipes fit into that format, then this project is for you. The storage area is large enough to hold cards that are 5 × 7 and larger, as well as magazine pages that are folded in half. And as a bonus, we mounted a binder clip to the inside face of the flip-up top so you can display recipe cards while you cook or bake.

The ½"-thick aspen used in this project can be found in most building centers in the shelving or molding section.

CONSTRUCTION MATERIALS

Quantity	Lumber
1	½ × 6" × 6' aspen
1	½ × 8" × 3' aspen

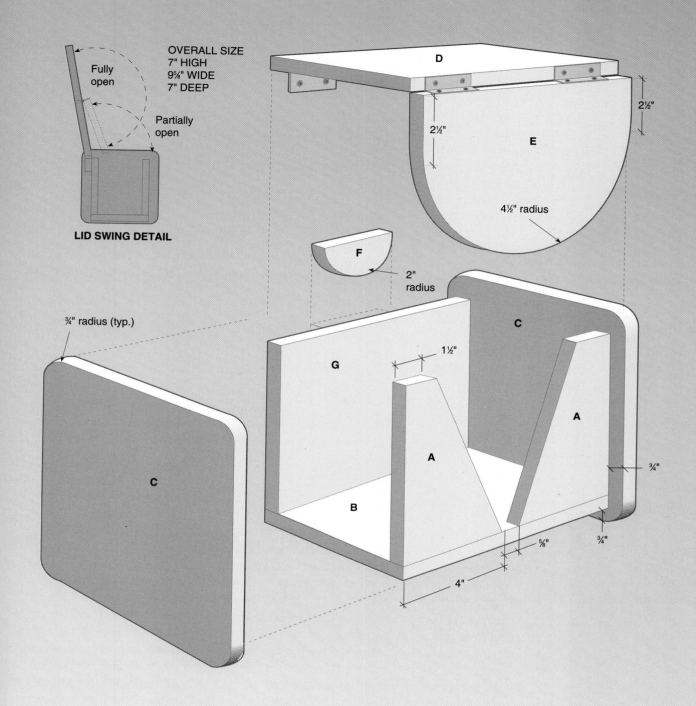

LID SWING DETAIL

Fully open

Partially open

OVERALL SIZE
7" HIGH
9⅝" WIDE
7" DEEP

¾" radius (typ.)

2½"

2½"

4½" radius

2" radius

1½"

¾"

⅝"

¾"

4"

		Cutting List		
Key	**Part**	**Dimension**	**Pcs.**	**Material**
A	Front	½ × 5½ × 4"	2	Aspen
B	Bottom	½ × 5½ × 8⅝"	1	Aspen
C	End	½ × 7 × 7"	2	Aspen
D	Lid	½ × 5½ × 8½"	1	Aspen

		Cutting List		
Key	**Part**	**Dimension**	**Pcs.**	**Material**
E	Top	½ × 5½ × 8½"	1	Aspen
F	Stop	½ × 1½ × 4"	1	Aspen
G	Back	½ × 5½ × 8⅝"	1	Aspen

Materials: Glue, 4d finish nails, 1 × 1½" butt hinges (4), #20 binder clip, #8 × ¾" roundhead sheet-metal screw, finishing materials.

Note: Measurements reflect the actual size of dimensional lumber.

Directions:
Recipe Box

MAKE THE FRONT, BACK & BOTTOM. Cut the fronts (A), back (G) and bottom (B) to size from ½"-thick stock (we used aspen, but you can substitute any solid wood material, or even plywood if you plan to paint the recipe box or you don't mind attaching veneer tape to all the edges before staining and topcoating it). Draw tapered cutting lines on the fronts: start the lines 1½" in from one corner at the top end, and connect them to the opposite bottom corner (see *Diagram*, page 33). Cut along these lines with a jig saw or circular saw to form the fronts **(photo A).** Sand the fronts, back and bottom with medium (100- or 120-grit) sandpaper to smooth out the rough spots, then finish-sand them with fine (150- or 180-grit) sandpaper.

ASSEMBLE THE FRONT, BACK & BOTTOM. When attaching these, and all other parts in the recipe box, drill pilot holes before nailing to prevent the wood from splitting. All the parts in this section are attached with glued butt joints. Use clamps to keep the pieces stationary during assembly. Glue the edges and fasten the back to the bottom by driving 1" brads up through the bottom and into the bottom edge of the back. Make sure the edges are flush. Set the brads with a nail set to eliminate any exposed nail heads. Next, attach the fronts to the

TIP

Most dimension lumber sold at building centers is 1" thick (¾" thick actual). But as wood becomes more scarce, the availability of thinner stock is increasing. Check in the shelving or molding sections for a wider variety of thinner wood, as well as smaller plywood "handy panels" with a variety of wood veneer surfaces.

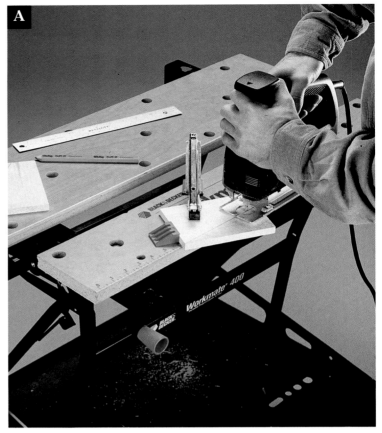

After drawing a tapered cutting line on each front, use a jig saw to cut the fronts to shape.

bottom using the same method **(photo B).** The space between the front pieces will form an open "V" with a ⅝"-wide gap between the pieces where they meet the bottom. Measure between the fronts and the back at several points to make sure the pieces are squarely positioned on the bottom. Smooth out sharp edges on the pieces with sandpaper.

BUILD THE ENDS. Start by cutting the ends (C) to size. Set the legs of a compass to draw a ¾" radius, then use it to mark roundovers at all corners of each end. Cut the roundovers with a jig saw, then sand them smooth. For uniform results, clamp the ends together and sand the roundovers smooth

as if the parts were one board. Finish-sand the ends. Using a combination square as a straightedge, draw a line ¾" in from the front and the back edge on the inside face of each end—these lines mark positions for the back and fronts of the box. Make sure the lines are parallel to the edges of the end panels. Use the combination square to draw a third line on each end, ¼" up from the bottom edges **(photo C).** This third line marks the bottom position.

ATTACH THE SIDES. Glue the edges of the front, bottom and back pieces, then align them at the reference lines on the ends. Drive 1" brads through the ends and into the joining edges of the bottom, fronts and back.

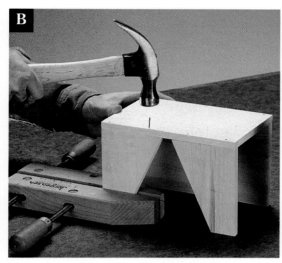

Attach the fronts to the bottom by driving 4d finish nails through the bottom into the front edges. Make sure the side and front edges are flush.

Use a combination square to mark positions for the bottom, back, and fronts onto the inside faces of the sides.

Finish-sand all parts with 150- or 180-grit sandpaper, and smooth out any sharp edges.

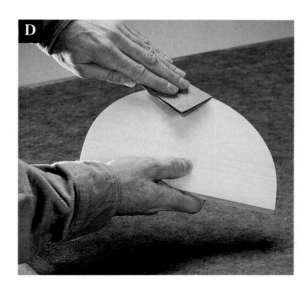

MAKE THE LID & TOP. The lid and top make up a two-part assembly that flips up to a near vertical position when the box is opened. The parts are hinged together so the top folds flat against the front of the box when the box is closed. The inside face of the top is fitted with a binder clip that can hold a recipe card while you prepare your food. Cut the lid (D) and top (E) to size. Use a compass to draw a semicircular cutting line with a 4½" radius centered at the bottom edge of the top. The ends of the cutting line should meet the sides of the top 2½" away from the top edge of the top. Cut along the cutting lines with a jig saw, then sand the curved edge smooth **(photo D).** With the lid and top cut to size and shape, join the pieces with a pair of evenly spaced 1 × 1½" butt hinges (we used brass hinges for a more decorative look). Fasten the hinges to the front edge of the lid and top edge of the top, about 1" in from each end. Use a #8 × ½" roundhead sheet metal screw to attach a #20 (small) binder clip to the inside face of the top. Center the screw for the binder clip about ⅜" away from the high point of the curve. Join the back edge of the lid to the top edge of the back with two 1 × 1½" butt hinges. The stop (F) is a semicircle with a 2" radius cut from ½"-thick material. Cut and finish-sand the stop. Use glue and nails to attach the stop to the outside face of the back, with the straight edge flush with the top of the back. The stop prevents the lid from opening too far past the vertical point.

APPLY THE FINISHING TOUCHES. Set all nail heads with a nail set, then fill the holes with wood putty. Finish-sand the surfaces. Finish the recipe box to match your kitchen decor. We used a natural shellac finish on our recipe box.

TIP

Binder clips are sold at office supply stores in a variety of sizes. Made of tempered steel, they are used to bind stacks of paper together if the stack is too thick for a paper clip.

Laundry Supply Cabinet

Get maximum use from a minimum of floor space with this laundry supply cabinet. Just slide it into a corner and store your laundry supplies without clutter.

This laundry supply cabinet can help keep notoriously messy rooms in check. Although it takes up a small amount of floor space, the tall cabinet is capable of holding a surprising amount of supplies—including a full-length ironing board. We installed a drop-down shelf at ironing board level and an interior shelf section to keep folded clothes, laundry detergent, bleach, dryer sheets—

everything you need to get the job done. On the door we put a handy storage box for anything from clothespins to spray bottles, and a hinged hanger arm for keeping that freshly pressed shirt out of your way while you work. A laundry organizer is one of the handiest projects you'll find. Nowhere in the home is storage so im-

portant (and so neglected) as in the laundry room. The narrow cabinet and fold-out features of this laundry room organizer are built for compact efficiency. You'll be surprised how much it will store, and how often you will use it. With an organizer like this, you may find the headache of doing laundry eased substantially.

CONSTRUCTION MATERIALS

Quantity	Lumber
2	¾" × 4 × 8' plywood
1	1 × 8" × 4' pine
1	1 × 6" × 4' pine
1	1 × 4" × 4' pine
1	1 × 2" × 8' pine
1	¾ × ¾" × 8' cove molding
1	¾ × ¾" × 8' base shoe molding
2	¾ × 1⅛" × 8' stop molding

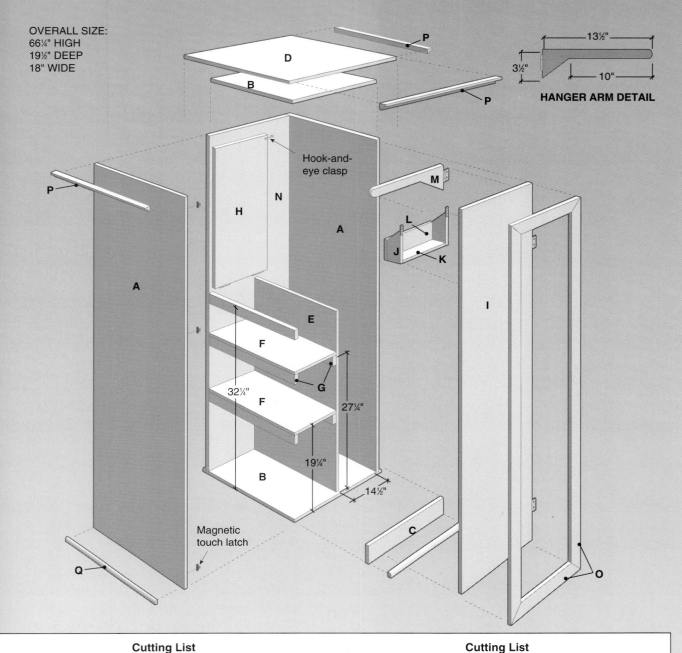

OVERALL SIZE:
66¼" HIGH
19½" DEEP
18" WIDE

Hook-and-eye clasp

Magnetic touch latch

13½"
3½"
10"

HANGER ARM DETAIL

32¼"
27¼"
19¼"
14½"

Key	Part	Dimension	Pcs.	Material
A	Side	¾ × 19 × 65½"	2	Plywood
B	End	¾ × 17½ × 18¼"	2	Plywood
C	Stringer	¾ × 1 × 17½"	1	Plywood
D	Cap	¾ × 20½ × 20½"	1	Plywood
E	Divider	¾ × 17½ × 32¼"	1	Plywood
F	Shelf	¾ × 10¼ × 17½"	2	Plywood
G	Cleat	¾ × 1½ × 17"	5	Pine
H	Drop-down shelf	¾ × 12 × 27¾"	1	Plywood
I	Door	¾ × 17 × 62¾"	1	Plywood

Cutting List

Key	Part	Dimension	Pcs.	Material
J	Box side	¾ × 3½ × 8"	2	Pine
K	Box bottom	¾ × 3½ × 10½"	1	Pine
L	Box front	¾ × 5½ × 12"	1	Pine
M	Hanger arm	¾ × 3½ × 13½"	1	Pine
N	Back	¾ × 16½ × 65½"	1	Plywood
O	Door frame	¾ × 1⅛" × *	4	Molding
P	Top frame	¾ × ¾" × *	3	Molding
Q	Base frame	¾ × ¾" × *	3	Molding

Materials: Glue, utility hinges (1½ × 3", 1½ × 1½"), 1" brads, wood screws (#6 × 1¼", #6 × 2"), 3" brass mending plates (2), touch latches (2), hook-and-eye clasp, finishing materials.

Note: Measurements reflect the actual size of dimensional lumber.
*Cut to fit.

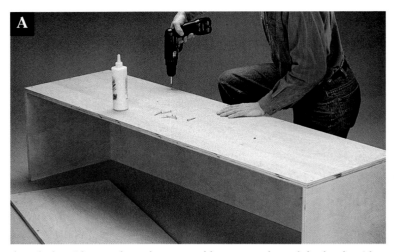

Attach the side panels to the top and bottom ends and the back with glue and wood screws.

Screw butt hinges into the back to secure the drop-down shelf to the cabinet.

Attach the stop molding to the door 1" from the top, bottom and side edges.

Directions:
Laundry Supply Cabinet

MAKE THE CABINET. If you plan and cut carefully, you can make all of the plywood parts for this project from two 4 × 8 sheets of plywood. Start by cutting the sides (A), ends (B) and back (N) to size. Sand all parts smooth with medium-grit sandpaper after cutting. Attach the back to the ends with glue and #6 × 2" wood screws driven through the back and into the ends. Make sure the edges are flush. Use glue and wood screws to attach the sides to the

back and ends **(photo A).** Make sure the side edges are flush with the back and ends.

ATTACH THE STRINGER & CAP. The cap is a square piece of plywood centered on top of the cabinet. The stringer is a thin strip that fits inside the cabinet along the bottom. Cut the stringer (C) and cap (D) to size. Center the cap over the top end, and fasten it with glue and counterbored #6 × 1¼" wood screws, driven up through the top end and into the cap. Attach the stringer between the sides at the bottom of the cabinet so that its front face is flush with the front edges. Glue the stringer, then drive #6 × 1¼" wood screws through the sides and bottom end to fasten it.

ATTACH THE DROP-DOWN SHELF. The drop-down shelf is attached to the back of the cabinet and can be easily folded up when not in use. Cut the drop-down shelf (H) to size. Measure and mark a line on the back (on the inside of the cabinet) 36¼" from the bottom. This line marks the position of the bottom edge of the drop-down shelf. Attach the

drop-down shelf at this line with 1½ × 1½" butt hinges **(photo B).** Make sure there is a ¼"-wide space between the side of the shelf and cabinet to allow room for the shelf to drop down. Install a hook-and-eye clasp on the cabinet back and the edge of the drop-down shelf to secure it in the upright position.

MAKE THE DOOR. The door (I) is cut to size and trimmed with stop molding. Start by cutting the door to size from ¾"-thick plywood. Use a straight-edge or square to draw guidelines 1" from the edges on the front face of the door. These guidelines mark the position of the outside edges of the door frame (O). Use a miter box to cut the stop molding at 45° angles to fit against these lines. Drill pilot holes, and attach stop molding to the door with 1" brads and glue **(photo C).**

MAKE THE SHELVES. The shelves (F) fit inside the cabinet and are fastened to a divider (E) and the side with cleats (G). Cut the divider, shelves and cleats to size. On the inside of the cabinet, draw lines on one side, 15¼", 28" and

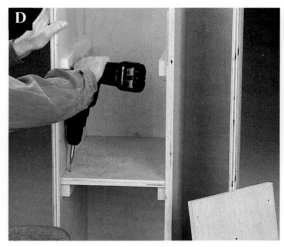

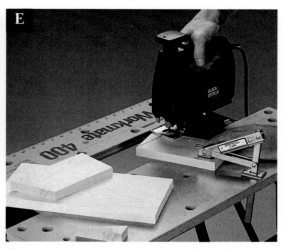

Attach the shelves by driving screws through the shelves into the cleats.

Draw angled cutting lines onto the box sides, then cut with a jig saw.

35¼" up from the bottom of the cabinet. These lines mark the position of the cleat tops, which support the shelves. Attach one cleat on each line with glue and #6 × 1¼" wood screws, then use the same methods to attach two cleats to the divider at 15¼" and 28" from its bottom edge. Make sure the cleats are square to the divider and side. To insert the divider, mark a line on the bottom end, 10¼" from the side with the cleats. Attach the divider with its shelf-side edge on this line with the cleats on the side and on the divider facing each other. You may want to test-fit the shelves at this time to make sure the divider is the proper distance from the side. Drive counterbored #6 × 1¼" wood screws through the stringer and back to attach the divider. Finally, attach the shelves to the divider by driving counterbored wood screws through the shelves and into the cleats **(photo D).**

MAKE THE BOX. A small box fits on the inside of the door and is attached with brass mending plates (small metal strips with screw holes for

fastening). Cut the box sides (J), box front (L) and box bottom (K) to size. Measure and mark a point 2½" down from one corner along one long side of each box side. Draw a cutting line from the opposite corner to this point, and cut it with a jig saw **(photo E).** Fasten the box bottom between the sides with glue and counterbored #6 × 1¼" wood screws, making sure the bottom and front edges are flush. Fasten the box front to the box bottom and sides, making sure the side and bottom edges are flush. Use brass mending plates to attach the box to the door so the box bottom is about 48" from the bottom of the door **(photo F).**

MAKE THE HANGER ARM. Cut the hanger arm (M) to shape according to the *Diagram* on page 37. Mount the hanger arm on the inside of the door with a butt hinge, making sure its top edge is 1" down from the top of the door. The hinged end of the hanger should be ¾" in from the door's side edge.

APPLY FINISHING TOUCHES. Hang the door with hinges mounted to the edge of the door and inside face of the

side. Use a miter box to cut top molding (P) to fit around the base of the cap, and base trim (Q) to fit around the bottom of the cabinet. Attach the molding with glue and 1" brads. Plug all counterbored holes with putty. Fill all plywood edges, and sand all the surfaces with medium (100- or 120-grit) sandpaper to smooth out the rough spots, then finish-sand with fine (150- or 180-grit) sandpaper. Prime and paint the laundry room organizer. Attach a magnetic touch latch at the top and bottom of the cabinet sides and door to hold the doors closed.

Use two brass mending plates to attach the box to the inside of the door.

Butcher Block Knife Box

Slice and dice on the oak-strip butcher block top, then store your kitchen knives in the handy drawer below.

The beauty of butcher block and the grace of simple design come together in this knife box. Strips of red oak are pinned and glued together to form a solid butcher block cutting board that functions as the top of the knife box. The low-profile drawer that fills the base of the box is sized to store a wide selection of kitchen knives in one convenient spot.

In this project, we show you how to glue and pin oak strips to create a butcher block surface—it's not as difficult as you may think. But if you aren't quite that ambitious, you may prefer to purchase a prefabricated butcher block panel cut to size. Or, you can even trim down a common cutting board to fit. If you choose to purchase the cutting board premade, try to find one that is made of red oak to match the wood used for the base and drawer. Other-

wise, you can purchase any top you want, but you'll get the best results if you change the wood type for the box and drawer, as well. Making your own butcher block panels is a valuable skill. Even if you are a little hesitant, we suggest that you give it a try. You can use the same techniques to create a multitude of handy kitchen accessories that are custom-designed to meet your needs. And after a few small projects, you may even want to tackle the ultimate butcher block project—making your own custom countertops.

CONSTRUCTION MATERIALS

Quantity	Lumber
6	1×2" $\times 8$' oak
1	1×3" $\times 6$' oak
1	1×4" $\times 6$' oak
1	$\frac{1}{4}$" $\times 4 \times 4$' oak

OVERALL SIZE:
4¼" HIGH
16½" WIDE
18" LONG

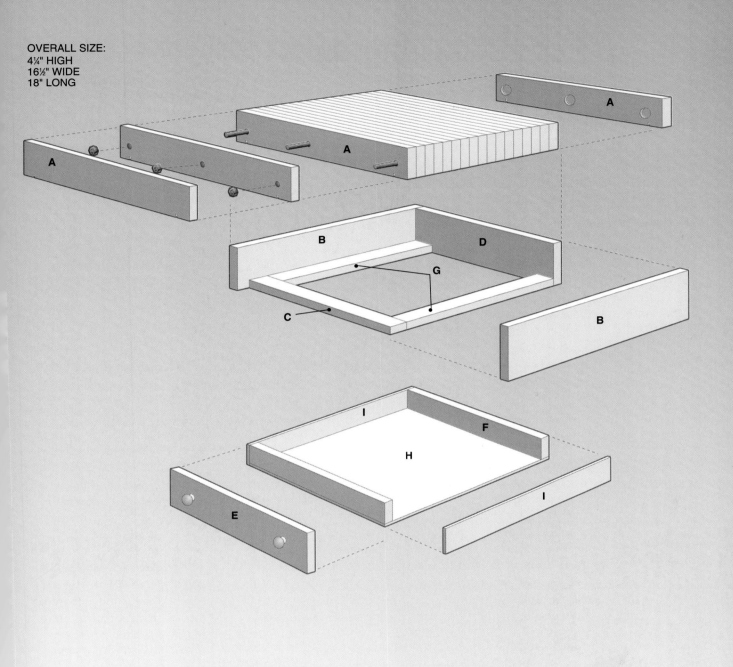

Cutting List				
Key	**Part**	**Dimension**	**Pcs.**	**Material**
A	Slat	¾ × 1½ × 18"	22	Oak
B	Side	¾ × 2¾ × 15½"	2	Oak
C	Front rail	¾ × 1½ × 15⅜"	1	Oak
D	Back	¾ × 2¾ × 15⅜"	1	Oak
E	Drawer front	¾ × 2½ × 15⅛"	1	Oak

Cutting List				
Key	**Part**	**Dimension**	**Pcs.**	**Material**
F	Drawer end	¾ × 1½ × 14⅛"	2	Oak
G	Drawer glide	¾ × 1½ × 12"	2	Oak
H	Drawer bottom	¼ × 15 × 13½"	1	Plywood
I	Drawer side	¾ × 1½ × 13½"	2	Oak

Materials: Glue, brass wood screws (#6 × 3", #6 × 2", #6 × 1¼"), 1" wire brads, ⅜"-dia. × 16" threaded rods (3) with nuts and washers, 1"-dia. wooden knobs (2), rubber bumpers, ⅜"-dia. oak plugs, finishing materials.

Note: Measurements reflect the actual size of dimensional lumber.

Directions:
Butcher Block Knife Box

PREPARE THE OAK SLATS. The butcher block cutting board is made from 22 oak slats that are glued together. The inner slats have three holes bored through them, positioned 2" from each end and at the center of each slat. During the gluing process, threaded rods are inserted into these holes and secured with nuts and washers to draw the slats together. The edge slats fit along the front and back of the butcher block, covering the ends of the threaded rods. Begin by cutting the slats (A) to length from 1 × 2 oak. Mark points 2" from both edge slat ends, and at each center. Use a drill fitted with a 1" spade bit and a portable drill guide to bore 1"-dia. × ½"-deep stopped holes at these points—on the inside face of each edge slat. Since you cannot use a depth stop with a spade bit, you should put a piece of tape ½" up on the bit to achieve the correct hole depth. If the point of the spade bit pokes through the slat, drill ⅜"-dia. holes through the slat holes. You can plug them later in the assembly process. Mark these corresponding points on one inner slat, and drill ⅛"-dia. pilot holes through this inside slat. You

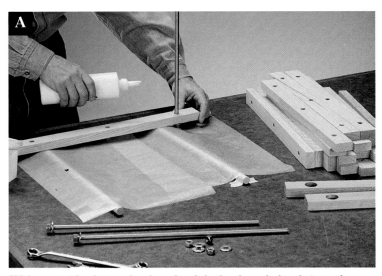

With an inside slat on the dowels, slide the threaded rods into place and apply a thin coat of glue to the inside face.

will use this slat as a drilling template for the remaining inner slats. It is extremely important to maintain accuracy during this portion of the process. Carefully clamp the drilled inner slat over an undrilled slat with their edges flush. Drill ⅛"-dia. holes through the holes in the drilled slat, into the undrilled slat. Remove the drilled inside slat and set it aside. Repeat these steps with the rest of the inner slats, then use a drill and portable drill guide to drill ½"-dia. holes through all the pilot holes at the centerpoints.

PREPARE THE WORKSURFACE. Since you will be gluing extensively as you assemble the cutting board, make sure your worksurface is adequately prepared. Start by taping two 1 × 2 spacers (we used 1"-dia. × 18"-long dowels) to a level worksurface, 12" apart. These pieces keep the cutting board off the worksurface as you assemble. Cover the worksurface with wax paper to prevent sticking and glue damage. Have the

threaded rods, washers and nuts ready.

ATTACH THE INNER SLATS. Place an inner slat on the dowels. Cut the three threaded rods to 16" lengths with a hacksaw. Use a grinding wheel or file to remove any burrs. Thread a nut and washer onto one end of the rod, and insert a threaded rod into a hole in the slat **(photo A).** Apply a thin coat of glue on the inside face. Apply glue to another inner slat and slide it over the rod and against the first slat. Continue the gluing process, gluing slats on both sides until all the inside slats are in place. Insert the remaining two rods into their holes. To ensure a flat surface, set a straight, square scrap piece across the slats. Tap the top of the piece with a hammer to make sure the slats are flat against the dowels or spacers on the underside. Slip the washers and nuts into place and tighten them until the glue squeezes out between the slats. Scrape the excess glue off the inner slats with a putty knife.

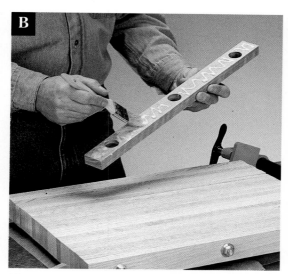

The two outer slats of the cutting board have 1"-dia. x ½"-deep holes to cover the ends of the rods.

Use a belt sander with a 100-grit sanding belt to create a smooth, even surface.

Use a circular saw and an edge guide to cut ⅛"-deep drip grooves ¼" from each bottom edge of the butcher block.

Let the glued-up assembly sit for ten minutes, then tighten the nuts.

ATTACH THE EDGE SLATS. The two edge slats fit over the front and back of the cutting board to cover the washers and nuts. They are attached with glue. Apply glue to the inside faces of the edge slats. Place the edge slats against the front and back of the inner slat assembly, making sure the holes cover the ends of the threaded rods **(photo B).** Clamp the slats together with a bar clamp until the glue is dry. Make sure bottoms of the slats are flush and even. Don't worry if the top of the butcher block surface is slightly uneven—you will probably need to sand this surface smooth. Allow the butcher block to dry for at least two days before continuing to the next step.

COMPLETE THE CUTTING BOARD. Use a belt sander with a 100-grit sanding belt to remove excess glue and smooth out the surface of the cutting board **(photo C).** If you don't own a belt sander, you can use a plane or finish sander to smooth out the cutting board. Use a circular saw with an edge guide to cut drip grooves on the bottom of the cutting board **(photo D).** Set the saw to cut ⅛"-deep grooves, ¼" from each edge of the block. Drip grooves help to protect the drawer section from spills because liquid trickling over the cutting board gets stopped. Sand the butcher block surfaces with 120-grit sandpaper and smooth out any rough edges.

MAKE THE BASE. The base fits under the butcher block cutting board. It includes a small drawer for convenient knife storage. Start by cutting the sides (B), front rail

Drive counterbored wood screws through the sides to secure the drawer glides to the bottom inside edges of the frame.

Use a portable drill guide to make sure the pilot holes in the sides are straight.

(C) and back (D) to size. Rip-cut the sides and back to a 2¾" width with a circular saw and cutting guide. Drill pilot holes through the sides (B) in position to fasten the back and front rail with #6 × 2" wood screws. Position the back between the two sides, inset ¼" from the back edges. Position the front edge of the front rail 1" from the front ends of the sides. Drill centered pilot holes in the front rail, ⅜" above the bottom edges of the sides. Drill centered pilot holes for the back ⅝" from the back ends of the sides. Sand the pieces with medium (100- or 120-grit) sandpaper to smooth out any rough spots, then finish-sand with fine (150- or 180-grit) sandpaper. Fasten the sides, front rail and back with glue and wood screws, making sure their bottoms are flush. Cut the drawer glides (G) to fit between the back and front rail. Finish-sand the pieces, then apply glue to their edges. Position the glides

To attach the drawer bottom, drive brads through the drawer bottom into the drawer sides and ends.

against the inside faces of the sides, flush with the bottom side edges. Secure the drawer glides by driving evenly spaced, counterbored #6 × 1¼" wood screws through the sides and back into the drawer glide edges **(photo E).** Finally, use a

drill with a portable drill guide to bore two evenly spaced pilot holes through the bottom edges of the sides. These pilot holes will be used later to fasten the bottom to the butcher block **(photo F).**

BUILD THE KNIFE DRAWER PARTS. We used a simple drawer design that requires few

Attach the drawer front to the drawer end with glue and wood screws driven through the drawer end.

To attach the base to the cutting board, drive wood screws through the pilot holes in the sides and into the cutting board.

parts. Start by cutting the drawer front (E), drawer ends (F), drawer sides (I) and drawer bottom (H) to size. Drill two evenly spaced pilot holes through one drawer end for attaching the drawer front. Sand the parts to smooth out any rough edges.

ASSEMBLE THE KNIFE DRAWER. Apply glue to the drawer ends, and attach the drawer sides by driving 1" brass brads through the sides and into the drawer ends. Apply glue to the bottoms of the drawer ends and drawer sides, then fasten the drawer bottom with 1" brass brads driven into the drawer sides and ends **(photo G).** Next, draw a line across the inside face of the drawer front, ½" from the bottom edge. This line will help you align the drawer front against the drawer box. Center a drawer end on the drawer front, with the bottom of the drawer end on the guideline. Drive evenly spaced,

counterbored #6 × 1¼" wood screws through the drawer end and into the drawer front to complete the drawer assembly **(photo H).** Smooth out the sharp edges with sandpaper, then attach drawer knobs on the drawer front, centered top-to-bottom, 4" from each end.

APPLY THE FINISHING TOUCHES. Fill all counterbored screw holes with ⅜"-dia. red oak plugs. Sand all the surfaces with medium (100- or 120-grit) sandpaper to smooth out rough spots, then finish-sand with fine (150- or 180-grit) sandpaper. Apply a food-safe finish to all the parts. We used salad bowl oil, a nontoxic finish good for any surface that comes in contact with food. In addition, the finish can be renewed easily as the butcher block surface becomes worn—simply sand out any knife marks, and reapply the salad-bowl oil. To improve the operation of the drawer,

apply several coats of beeswax to the tops of the front rail and drawer glides. Renew this wax as needed. Finally, fasten the base section to the butcher block by driving #6 × 3" wood screws through the pilot holes in the sides into the butcher block **(photo I).** Attach rubber bumpers to the bottom of the base section for stability and to protect your kitchen counter surfaces.

TIP

Line the bottom of the drawer with felt to protect both the knives and the drawer. Just cut a piece of felt to fit on the drawer bottom, and glue it in place.

Car Care Center

*Stash messy car maintenance products
in one compact unit.*

CONSTRUCTION MATERIALS

Quantity	Lumber
1	¼" × 2 × 4' tileboard
1	¾" × 4 × 8' ABX plywood
2	1 × 2" × 8' pine
1	1"-dia. × 24" pine dowel

Routine car maintenance is a messy activity involving oil, grime and even hazardous chemicals. Building and using a car care center is a good way to keep the mess of car maintenance concentrated in one spot.

This car care center has a shelf or bin that is designed to accommodate just about any product you put into or onto your car. Included in the design are: an optional sliding shelf for funnels with a shelf for an oil pan below; a tall shelf for antifreeze and other products sold in tall containers; a towel rod for drying rags; and a separate storage compartment that can be fitted with a locking hasp for potentially hazardous items.

OVERALL SIZE:
48" HIGH
18" WIDE
18" LONG

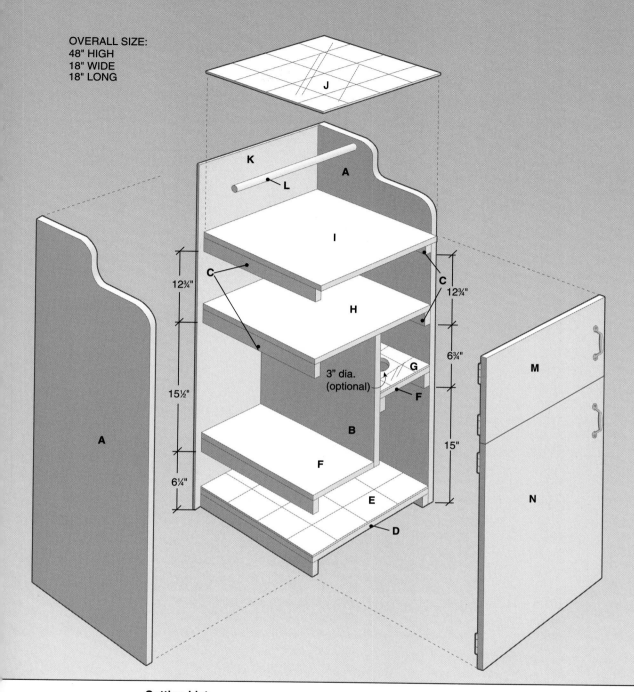

Cutting List

Key	Part	Dimension	Pcs.	Material
A	Side panel	¾ × 18 × 48"	2	Plywood
B	Center partition	¾ × 18 × 15½"	1	Plywood
C	Cleat	¾ × 1½ × 18"	9	Pine
D	Bottom panel	¾ × 16½ × 18"	1	Plywood
E	Tile cover	¼ × 16½ × 18"	1	Tileboard
F	Bin bottom	¾ × 7⅞ × 18"	2	Plywood
G	Tile cover	¼ × 7⅞ × 18"	1	Tileboard

Cutting List

Key	Part	Dimension	Pcs.	Material
H	Shelf	¾ × 16½ × 18"	1	Plywood
I	Worksurface	¾ × 16½ × 19"	1	Plywood
J	Tile cover	¼ × 16½ × 19"	1	Tileboard
K	Back panel	¼ × 18 × 48"	1	Plywood
L	Towel rod	1"-dia. × 18"	1	Pine
M	Shelf door	¾ × 18 × 11¾"	1	Plywood
N	Bin door	¾ × 18 × 24"	1	Plywood

Materials: Wood glue, #8 × 1¼" wood screws, wood putty, 2 × 2" butt hinges (4), door pulls (2), glide feet (4), and finishing materials.

Note: Measurements reflect the actual size of dimensional lumber.

Lay out the curved corners on the top end of the side panel and cut them out with a jig saw.

Mark the shelf cleat positions on the side panels and the center partition, following the spacing shown in the Diagram on page 47.

Directions:
Car Care Center

MAKE THE SIDE PANELS, CENTER PARTITION & CLEATS. Cut the side panels (A) for the car care center to size from ¾"-thick plywood. Lay out cutting lines at the top of each side panel: measure 10" from the back, across the top edge, and draw an 8"-long line; measure 9" down the front edge, from the top, and draw a 7"-long line; use a can with a diameter of about 4" to round over the corners where the cutting lines meet, as well as the front edge of the cutout (see Diagram, page 47). Cut out the contours with a jig saw **(photo A)**, then sand the edges of the cutout until smooth. Use the cutout as a template to draw cutting lines on the second side panel. Next, cut the center partition (B) to size and sand its edges and surfaces. Mark lines across the inside surfaces of the side panels at the appropriate cleat locations for each

Fasten the shelf cleats to the side panels and center partition with wood glue and wood screws.

side panel (see Diagram, page 47). Transfer the cleat locations to each side of the center partition, using a framing square to make sure the lines are straight and perpendicular to the edges of the panels **(photo B).** Make sure the bottoms of the partition and the side panel are aligned. Cut the shelf cleats (C) from 1 × 2 pine and attach them to the side panels and center partition at the marked locations, using wood glue and counterbored #6 × 1¼" wood screws **(photo C).**

ASSEMBLE THE SHELVES & SIDE PANELS. Cut the bottom panel (D), bin bottoms (F) and shelf (H). Stand the side panels upright and place the bottom panel on the bottom cleats. Fasten the bottom panel to the cleats with glue and screws. Cut a 6¼"-long spacer and stand it on the bottom panel to support the lower bin bottom while you attach it to the cleat on the left side panel. Then, fasten the center partition to the bin bottom, keeping the bottom edges flush, with glue and screws driven through the partition and into the edge of the bin bottom. Use at least three screws. Set the upper bin bottom onto the cleats. If you use funnels to change the fluid in your car, do not attach this shelf permanently. Then, after you attach the tile cover, cut out a 3"-dia. hole in the center to hold funnels. Simply slide out the shelf to insert the funnel—be sure to place an oil pan below to catch the drips. But if you do not use funnels, go ahead and attach the bin bottom to the cleats, and don't bother cutting the hole in the center. Attach the full-width shelf (H) to the cleats on the side panels, then drive two or three screws through the shelf and down into the top edge of the partition **(photo D)**. Cut the worksurface (I) and attach it to the top cleats.

INSTALL THE TILE COVERS. Cut tile covers (E, G, J) from a sheet of ⅛"-thick tileboard. Fasten them to the bottom panel, lower bin bottom, and worksurface, respectively. Use panel adhesive or tileboard adhesive to attach the tileboard **(photo E).** Set the tileboard by rolling it with an old rolling pin or a J-roller. If you plan to use the upper bin bottom for a funnel, cut a 3"-dia. hole in the center.

ATTACH THE DOORS & BACK PANEL. Cut the back (K) to size from ¼"-thick hardboard and fasten in place with 1" wire nails driven into the back edges of the cabinet. Cut the shelf door (M) and bin door (N). Attach two utility hinges to each door and hang the doors, making sure the space between the doors falls over the front edge of the full-width shelf.

APPLY FINISHING TOUCHES. Cut a 1"-dia. dowel to 18" in length to use as a towel rod (L). Drill 1"-dia holes for the dowel in the side panels, 2" down from the top edge and 5" in from the back on each panel. Insert the rod through the holes so the ends are flush with the outside surfaces of the panels. Pull the rod out slightly and apply glue to the ends, then reinsert the ends into the holes. Tack glide feet to the underside of the bottom panel. Fill screw counterbores and exposed plywood edges with wood putty, then sand all surfaces smooth. Apply paint or a protective topcoat. Attach a door pull to each door, and add a locking hasp to the cabinet door if desired.

Attach the full-width shelf to the partition.

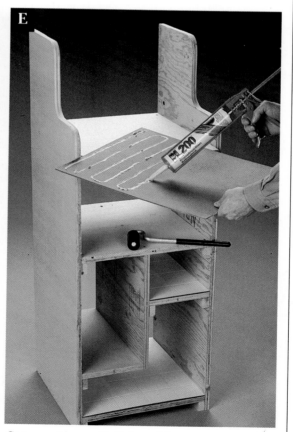

Cover surfaces with tileboard for easy cleanup.

Bread Box

Reduce the clutter on your countertop and add some country charm to your kitchen with this combination bread box and toaster garage.

CONSTRUCTION MATERIALS

Quantity	Lumber
1	1 × 8" × 8' oak
1	1 × 14 to16" × 4' oak panel

Add a down-home feeling to your kitchen with this uniquely styled combination bread box and toaster garage. Reminiscent of antique bread boxes, our design is updated to include a storage space for your toaster and a removable cutting board. The cutting board fits against the front of the bread box, con-cealing the toaster, and is held in place by the closed lid. Position the bread box close to an electrical outlet and pull the toaster out to use it, then tuck it back inside the bread box when you're finished. The cutting board works well as a preparation area and also as a crumb catcher to help keep cleanup time to a minimum.

OVERALL SIZE
17" HIGH
8¼" WIDE
18" LONG

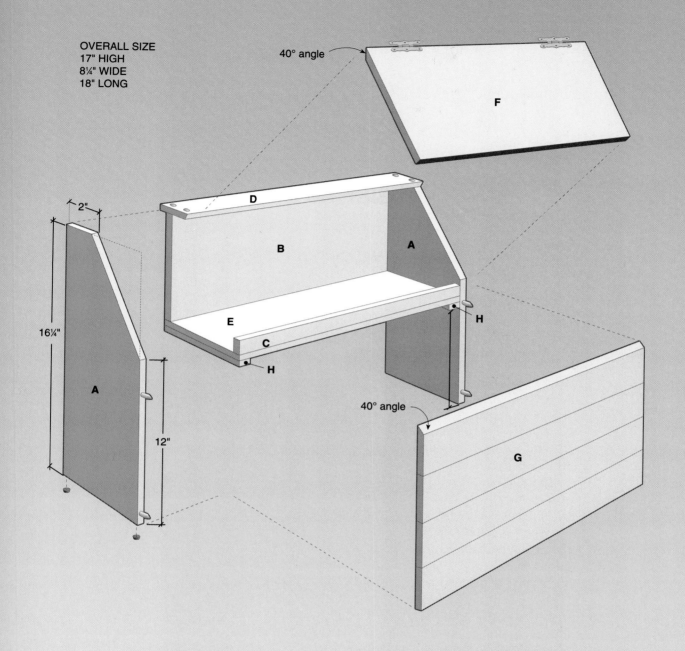

40° angle

F

2"

D

B

A

16¼"

E

A

C

H

12"

40° angle

H

G

Cutting List

Key	Part	Dimension	Pcs.	Material
A	Side	¾ × 7¼ × 16¼"	2	Oak
B	Back	¾ × 7¼ × 16½"	1	Oak
C	Front lip	¾ × 1½ × 16½"	1	Oak
D	Top	¾ × 2¼ × 18"	1	Oak

Cutting List

Key	Part	Dimension	Pcs.	Material
E	Bread shelf	¾ × 7¼ × 16½"	1	Oak
F	Lid	¾ × 9 × 18"	1	Oak
G	Cutting board	¾ × 12 × 18"	1	Oak
H	Cleat	¾ × 1 × 7¼"	2	Oak

Materials: Wood glue, #6 x 1¼" brass wood screws, (4) ⅜"-dia. wood table pins, 4 rubber glide feet.

Specialty items: Hand plane, preglued oak panels.

Note: Measurements reflect the actual size of dimensional lumber.

Use a circular saw to trim off corners at the tops of both side pieces.

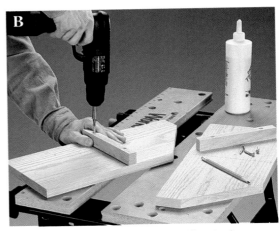

Fasten the cleats for the bread shelf to the box sides, using wood glue and brass screws.

Directions: Bread Box

MAKE THE SIDES. The sides of the bread box are simple rectangles with one corner removed to create a surface for the lid that slopes down from back to front. Start by cutting the sides (A) from 1 × 8 oak. Mark the endpoints for the tapered trim lines by measuring in 2" from a corner along the top edge of each side, then measuring down 12" from the same corner. Connect the endpoints, then cut at the line with a circular saw **(photo A).** Sand all edges and surfaces smooth. Cut the shelf cleats (H). On the inside surfaces of the sides, measure down 8" from the tops. Place the cleats in position and drill countersunk pilot holes through the cleats into the sides. Fasten the cleats to the sides with glue and #6 × 1¼" wood screws **(photo B).**

ASSEMBLE THE BOX. The sides, back, front and bread shelf form the basic box construction. Cut the bread shelf (E). Using glue and screws, fasten the bread shelf between the sides so it rests on the side cleats. Cut the back (B), and

Apply glue to the bottom and ends of the back, then fasten it to the box sides with brass wood screws.

attach it between the sides, with its bottom edge resting on the bread shelf **(photo C).** Make sure the back is flush with the back edges of the sides. Use glue and screws driven through the sides and into the ends of the back. Counterbore the pilot holes to accept oak plugs (usually ⅜"-dia.). Cut the front lip (C), and set it on the bread shelf, between the sides and flush with the front edge of the shelf. Drill counterbored pilot holes through the sides into the front lip and fasten in place with wood glue and screws.

MAKE THE LID & CUTTING BOARD. The lid and cutting board are wider than standard oak board widths. To make these parts, you can either edge-glue several strips of oak together (a relatively difficult operation that requires a lot of belt-sander work), or you can purchase preglued oak panels. Preglued panels are sold in several widths, from 14 to 24". They are solid hardwood (as opposed to plywood) so they are still good materials to use for cutting-board projects. Cut the lid (F) and cutting board (G) to length from an oak

Cut 40° bevels on one edge of the lid, the top and the cutting board using a circular saw.

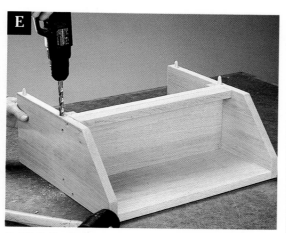

Drill ⅜"-dia. holes in the front edges of the sides for the table pins that hold the cutting board in place.

panel. The top (D) is only 2¼" wide when finished, but the bevel cut on the front edge will be much easier to make on a wider board, so you will be better off cutting it from a piece of 1 × 6 or 1 × 8. The top edge of the cutting board, the front edge of the top and the back edge of the lid are cut with bevels that match the slope of the sides. Set your circular saw to make a 40° bevel cut. Make a test cut on a piece of scrap wood first to make sure the angle matches the side profile, then use a straightedge guide to bevel-cut the back edge of the lid **(photo D).** Also bevel-cut the top edge of the cutting board and the front edge of the top. When cut, the taller side of the lid should measure 9", and the taller side of the cutting board should be 12".

ATTACH THE TOP, LID & CUT-TING BOARD. The top strip is attached to the tops of the side and the back with screws. It supports the lid, which is attached to it with hinges. The cutting board is fitted over four table pins that are mounted in the front edges of the sides. When the lid is closed, it holds the cutting board in place.

Position the top on the side panels, flush with the outside surfaces of the sides. Drill counterbored pilot holes through the top into the top edges of the sides, and fasten with glue and #6 × 1¼" brass wood screws. Drill a pair of ⅜"-dia. holes in the front edge of each side 1" and 8" up from the bottom. The holes should be deep enough so ⅜" of the table pins will protrude out when the pins are inserted **(photo E).** Apply glue to the blunt ends of the table pins and tap them into the holes with a wood or rubber mallet. Attach brass butt hinges to the lid, 2½" in from

each end, then attach the top to the hinges. Rub chalk on the points of the table pins and place the cutting board in position against the pins to mark the hole locations **(photo F).** Drill ⅜"-dia. × ⅜"-deep holes in the cutting board at the corresponding locations.

APPLY FINISHING TOUCHES. Apply glue and insert button plugs in the screw hole counterbores. Finish-sand the entire bread box. Apply several coats of salad bowl oil for a nontoxic protective finish. Fasten rubber glide feet to the four bottom corners of the bread box.

Rub chalk on the points of the table pins and press the cutting board in position against the pins to mark drilling locations on the cutting board.

Toy Drop-box

Designed to look like a mailbox and work like a toy chest, this fun project will fascinate your kids and inspire them to keep their favorite toys where they belong.

The design for this toy chest was based on the idea that the more interesting a child finds a piece of furniture, the more likely he or she is to use it. In addition to the striking appearance based on a postal drop-box, this toy chest has two loading points, one at the top and one at the front, to make it more interactive for your child. Soft toys can be dropped into the top opening, but more fragile playthings can be loaded carefully through the front opening. Self-closing hinges on the front ensure that the door stays closed, without the hazards created by latches that cannot be operated from inside. Rounded corners on the hinged top lid are very forgiving if they get bumped by a child.

Your kids will love this toy drop-box because it is fun and interactive. You will love it because it is easy and inexpensive to make. The entire project is constructed from two sheets of plywood—we used birch plywood because it has smooth, splinter-free surfaces that are excellent for painting. The rounded tops of the toy drop-box sides are easy to mark and cut, and even the rail structure that supports the hinged lid is very easy to make and install.

We painted our toy drop-box blue to stay with the postal box theme. But the broad flat surfaces present many options if you decide to be more creative: sponge painting or applying colorful decals are just two of the possibilities.

CONSTRUCTION MATERIALS

Quantity	Lumber
1	¾" × 4 × 8' birch plywood
1	¾" × 4 × 4' birch plywood

OVERALL SIZE:
48" HIGH
24" WIDE
25½" LONG

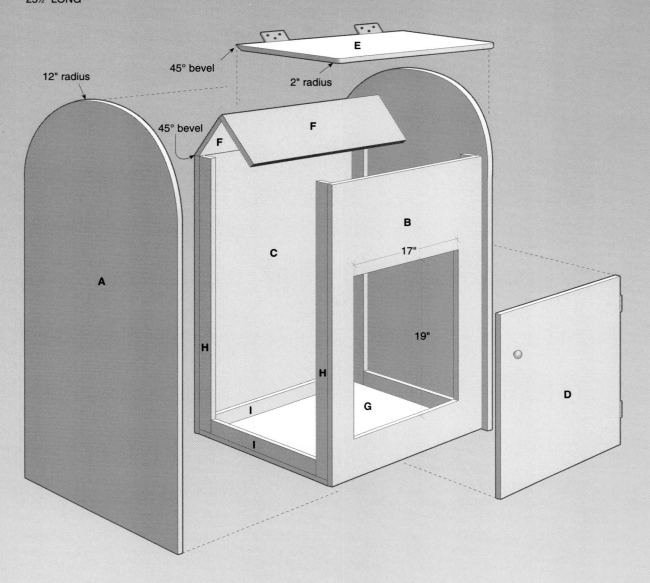

12" radius

45° bevel

2" radius

45° bevel

E

F

F

F

A

C

B

17"

19"

H

H

I

G

I

D

Cutting List

Key	Part	Dimension	Pcs.	Material
A	Side panel	¾ × 24 × 48"	2	Plywood
B	Front panel	¾ × 24 × 37½"	1	Plywood
C	Back panel	¾ × 24 × 37½"	1	Plywood
D	Door	¾ × 18 × 20"	1	Plywood
E	Lid	¾ × 14 × 23¾"	1	Plywood

Cutting List

Key	Part	Dimension	Pcs.	Material
F	Top rail	¾ × 7½ × 24"	2	Plywood
G	Bottom panel	¾ × 1½ × 17½"	1	Plywood
H	Side cleat	¾ × 1 × 36¾"	4	Plywood
I	Bottom cleat	¾ × 1 × 19½"	2	Plywood

Materials: Wood glue, #6 × 1¼" wood screws, wood filler, hinges, finishing materials, nail-on glide feet.

Note: Measurements reflect the actual size of dimensional lumber.

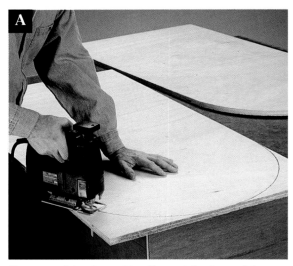

Draw semicircular cutting lines at the tops of the side panels, then cut with a jig saw.

Lay out the side and bottom cleat positions on the side panels, then attach the cleats with wood glue and screws.

Draw the rectangular cutout for the front door opening on the front panel, then drill a starter hole and make the cutout with a jig saw.

Directions: Toy Drop-Box

BUILD THE SIDE PANELS. The side panels have rounded tops that are cut with a jig saw, and the inside surfaces are cleated to create screwing surfaces for the other parts of the basic box construction. Cut the side panels (A). On one of the panels, measure down 12" from the top edge and 12" in from the side, then mark a point. Drive a finish nail at this point, then tie a string to the nail. Tie a pencil to the string, 12" out from the nail, pull the string taut, and draw a sweeping semicircle from side to side to make the cutting line for the top roundover. Cut along the line with a jig saw, then sand the cut smooth. Use this side panel as a template to mark a matching cutting line on the other side panel, then cut and sand the second side panel **(photo A).** To ensure that the sides are completely uniform, clamp them together face to face so the tops are as closely aligned as possible. Sand both roundovers at the same time with a power sander until they are shaped exactly alike. Trim all edges with a router and a ¼" roundover bit, or use a power sander to smooth out the sharp edges. Cut the side cleats (H) and bottom cleats (I). On the inside surfaces of the side panels, lay out the locations for the cleats. The vertical side cleats should be placed 1¼" in from the front and back edges of the side panels. This will allow for a ½" setback once the front and back panels are installed. The bottom cleats should be ¾" up from the bottoms of the side panels to allow room for the bottom panel. Attach the cleats with glue and #6 × 1¼" wood screws **(photo B).**

MAKE THE FRONT, BACK & BOTTOM PANELS. Cut the front panel (B), back panel (C) and bottom panel (G) to size from birch plywood. On the front panel, lay out a 17 × 19" door opening, 5" up from the bottom and 3½" in from each side. Drill a ⅜"-dia. starter hole on the inside of each corner, then cut the opening with a jig saw **(photo C).** Sand all the edges smooth.

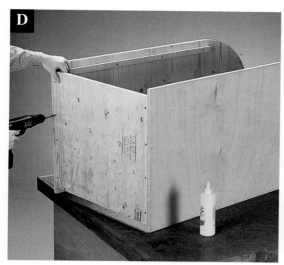
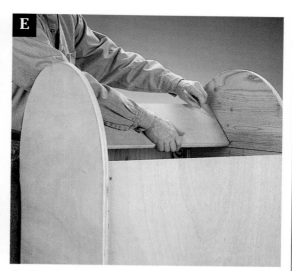

Fasten the bottom panel to the bottom cleats on the side panels.

Outline the top rail assembly for reference, then fasten it with glue and screws.

ASSEMBLE THE BOX. To assemble the box components (the front, sides, back and bottom panels), simply arrange the parts together so the front and back match up with the cleats on the inside surfaces of the side frame. Then, fasten the parts together with glue and wood screws—be sure to counterbore the screw pilot holes slightly so they can be filled with wood putty to cover the screw heads. Cut the bottom panel (G) and fasten it to the undersides of the bottom cleats—it should fit snugly inside the front, sides, and back **(photo D).**

MAKE & INSTALL THE TOP RAILS. The top rails are butted together at the top of the toy drop-box, where they fit against the sides in an inverted "V" position. Their function is largely decorative, but the front rail does support the hinges for the lid. Cut the top rails (F) to size: on one of the rails (to be used in the back position), cut a 45° bevel at the back edge. The bevel fits against the top edge of the back panel. Butt the two rails together to form a V-shape,

with the beveled edge away from the joint. Join the rails with glue and screws. Now, draw reference lines across the inside faces of the side panels, connecting the top edges of the front and back panels. Position the rail assembly so the beveled edge is flat against the top edge of the back panel, and the other free end is flush against the reference lines on the side panels **(photo E).** Drill counterbored pilot holes through the centers of the outlines, then attach the rail assembly with glue and screws.

ATTACH THE LID & DOOR. Cut the lid (E) and the door (D) to size from plywood, cutting a 45° bevel on the rear edge of the lid so it opens and closes without contacting the top rails. Use a compass to mark a 2"-radius roundover at the outside corners of the lid. Smooth out sharp edges on the lid and door using a router with a ¼" roundover bit, or a power sander. Fasten butt hinges to the lid, 2" in from each end, then mount the lid to the front edge of the top rail assembly. Mount the front door to the

front panel with self-closing hinges, allowing for a ½" overlap on all sides of the door opening **(photo F).**

APPLY FINISHING TOUCHES. Fill all counterbores and exposed plywood edges with wood putty. Sand smooth and apply your finish of choice (we used blue enamel paint). Attach nail-on glide feet to the bottoms of the side panels, and attach a door pull to the front door.

Attach the front door to the front panel with self-closing hinges, positioning the door with a ½" overhang on all sides.

Rolling Tool Cart

Part storage cabinet, part sawhorse, the tool locker allows you to wheel your tools right to the job site.

Put a stop to those endless tool-fetching trips from your garage to your work site with this rolling tool cart. Big enough to hold all the tools you'll need for just about any job or project, the rolling tool cart also doubles as a sturdy worksurface. The cutouts on the top create clearance for long boards, and the four corners of the top give ample support to full-size sheet goods. When you're not using the top as a worksurface, the ends make a convenient holding area for clamps. With four sturdy casters and cabinet doors that snap shut securely, this tool cart can be rolled along almost any surface without sending your valuable hand tools and portable power tools clattering to the ground. The rolling tool cart is made by attaching plywood panels to a 2 × 4 pine frame. With a little ingenuity and planning, all the plywood parts for this project can be cut from a single sheet of ¾"-thick plywood.

CONSTRUCTION MATERIALS

Quantity	Lumber
1	¾" × 4' × 8' plywood
3	2 × 4" × 8' pine

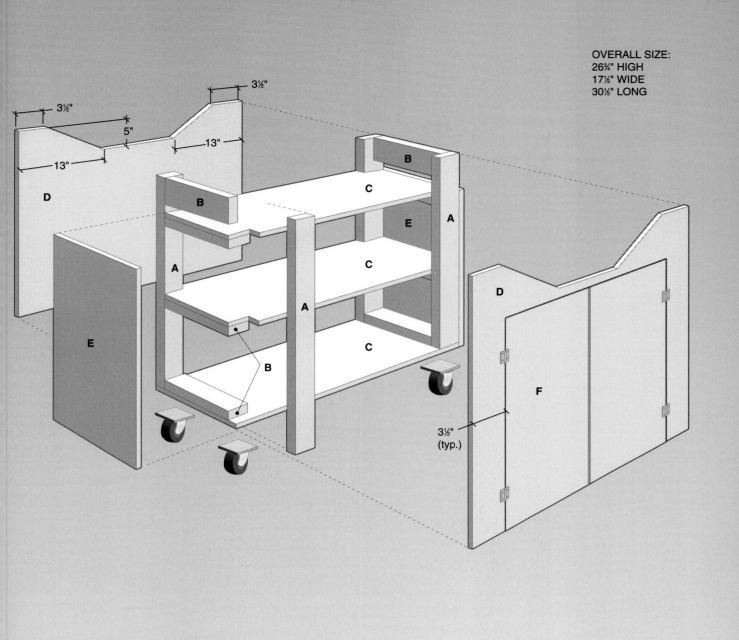

OVERALL SIZE:
26¾" HIGH
17½" WIDE
30½" LONG

3½"

3½"

5"

13"

13"

B

C

D

B

E

A

A

C

A

C

E

B

D

F

3½"
(typ.)

Cutting List

Key	Part	Dimension	Pcs.	Material
A	Post	1½ × 3½ × 26"	4	Pine
B	Rail	1½ × 3½ × 13"	8	Pine
C	Shelf	¾ × 16 × 30"	3	Plywood

Cutting List

Key	Part	Dimension	Pcs.	Material
D	Front, back	¾ × 30 × 26¾"	2	Plywood
E	End panel	¾ × 17½ × 21¾"	2	Plywood
F	Door	¾ × 11¼ × 20¾"	2	Plywood

Materials: Glue, 1½ × 3" butt hinges, double roller catches (2), 3"-dia. locking casters (4), wood screws (#6 × 2", #6 × 2½"), finishing materials.

Specialty Items: Straightedge guide, bar clamps, tape measure.

Note: Measurements reflect the actual size of dimensional lumber.

Fasten the rail between the posts with glue and wood screws.

Cut the cabinet shelves from a sheet of plywood, using a circular saw and straightedge guide.

Directions: Rolling Tool Cart

BUILD THE CABINET FRAMES. The rails are attached between sets of posts to form two frames that are the structural anchors for the project. Start by cutting the posts (A) and rails (B) to size. Sand these and all parts with medium-grit sandpaper after cutting. Clamp one rail between two posts ends, making sure their edges are flush. Fasten the pieces with glue and #6 × 2½" wood screws (photo A). Repeat this procedure with another rail-and-post pair. Mark reference lines for shelf locations 12" up from one end of the posts and 5¾" from the other end, across their inside faces. Position the rails on the reference lines so their top faces are on these lines, and fasten them with glue and wood screws. Fasten the top

Draw cutting lines for the front and back panels according to the Diagram on page 81.

rails between the posts with the top edges flush with the tops of the posts. The outside faces of these top rails should be flush with the outsides of the posts.

INSTALL SHELVES BETWEEN THE CABINET FRAMES. The rolling tool cart has a bottom shelf, a middle shelf, and a top worksurface. The middle shelf and the worksurface are notched at their corners to fit around the 2 × 4 posts. Cut the shelves (C) to size from ¾"-thick plywood (photo B), then cut 3½ × 1½" notches in the corners of two of the

shelves (see Diagram, page 81) so they fit around the posts. Use a jig saw to cut the corner notches. Attach the shelf without notches to the bottom ends of the cabinet frames. Make sure the ends with the higher shelf rails are joined to the base, flush with the ends. Use glue and #6 × 2" wood screws driven up through the base and into the bottom ends of the frames. Attach the notched shelves to the middle and upper sets of rails, using glue and screws.

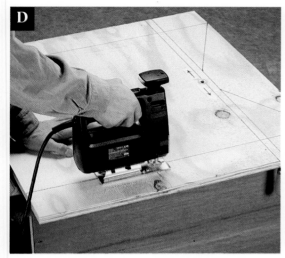

Use a jig saw to cut a 21 × 23" rectangle from the front face panel.

After making the V-shaped cutout, fasten the frames and back to the cabinet frame.

MAKE THE FRONT & BACK. The front and back parts of the cabinet start out the same size and shape, but the front panel is cut out in the center to make a face frame for the cabinet doors (which are made from the cutout plywood). Cut two pieces of plywood to size for the front and back (D). Mark cutting lines for the V-shaped cutout at the top of each piece (see *Diagram*, page 81). On one of the panels (this will be the front), draw cutting lines for the door cutout 3½" in from the sides and ¾" down from the bottom of the V-shaped cutout. This will create a cutout that is 23" wide and 21" high **(photo C).** Make the V-shaped cutouts in both workpieces with a jig saw, then sand the parts smooth. Make the door cutout on the front panel by cutting along the guidelines with a jig saw, forming a 23 × 21" rectangle **(photo D).** Cut carefully—the waste piece can be cut down the center to create the cabinet doors (F). Use glue and #6 × 2" wood screws to attach the panels at the front and

back **(photo E).** Save the cutout rectangle to make the doors (F).

MAKE THE ENDS. The ends (E) are same-sized plywood panels that are attached along the sides of the rolling tool cart. Cut the two panels to size,

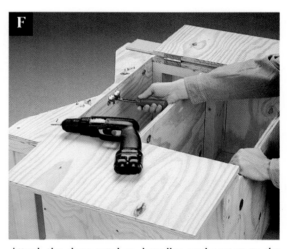

Attach the door catches, handles and casters to the rolling tool cart.

and use glue and #6 × 2" wood screws to attach the end panels with their top edges flush with the top shelf.

INSTALL THE DOORS. The cabinet doors are made from a 23 × 21"-high piece of plywood. If possible, use the cutout from the front panel. Use a circular saw to cut the doors to size. Sand their edges with a belt sander mounted on your worksurface, and attach them to the front panel with evenly spaced 1½ × 3" butt hinges, making sure to maintain a ¼"-wide gap between the panel frame and

the door edges and a ⅛"-wide gap between the doors.

APPLY FINISHING TOUCHES. Attach door handles and double roller door catches **(photo F),** and attach heavy-duty, 3" locking casters on the bottom of the posts. Make sure to center the casters on the posts to enable the tool cart to roll easily and smoothly. Locking casters are necessary if you want a stable workstation. Paint the project inside and out with a hard enamel paint.

Hardware Organizer

Turn your basement or garage into a mini-hardware store by stocking this organizer with a ready supply of hardware.

CONSTRUCTION MATERIALS

Quantity	Lumber
1	¾" × 4 × 8' plywood
1	2 × 6" × 6' pine

For most homeowners, weekend projects always seem to include several quick trips to the hardware store to buy a handful of screws, a pair of hinges, a few finish nails, or other common types of hardware that are forgotten in the initial shopping trip. You can eliminate most of those annoying trips by stocking up with a basic assortment of hardware. And with this roomy hardware organizer, you can store your hardware supply so the needed items are easy to find when the need arises. With the portable trays at the top of the organizer, you can load up all the hardware you need for a project and bring it right to the job site.

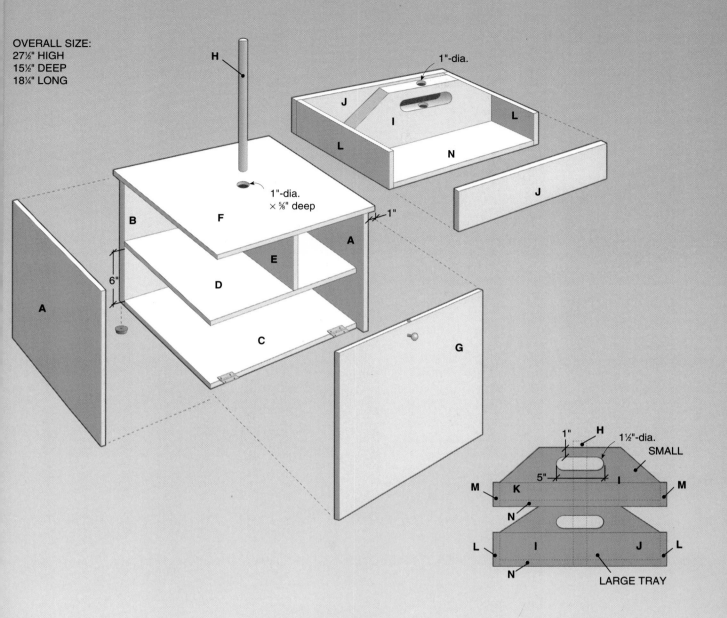

OVERALL SIZE:
27½" HIGH
15½" DEEP
18¼" LONG

H

1"-dia.

J

I

L

L

N

J

1"-dia.
× ⅝" deep

B

F

1"

A

6"

E

D

A

C

G

H

1"

1½"-dia.
SMALL

5"

I

M

K

M

N

L

I

J

L

N

LARGE TRAY

Cutting List				
Key	**Part**	**Dimension**	**Pcs.**	**Material**
A	Side	¾ × 13½ × 16"	2	Plywood
B	Back	¾ × 13½ × 17¾"	1	Plywood
C	Bottom	¾ × 15¼ × 17¾"	1	Plywood
D	Shelf	¾ × 15¼ × 17¾"	1	Plywood
E	Cabinet divider	¾ × 6 × 15¼"	1	Plywood
F	Top	¾ × 17 × 19¼"	1	Plywood
G	Door	¾ × 12⅝ × 19¼"	1	Plywood

Cutting List				
Key	**Part**	**Dimension**	**Pcs.**	**Material**
H	Dowel	1"-dia. × 14"	1	Hardwood
I	Tray divider	1½ × 5½ × 16½"	2	Pine
J	Tray side	¾ × 4 × 18"	2	Pine
K	Tray side	¾ × 2½ × 18"	2	Pine
L	Tray end	¾ × 4 × 14"	2	Pine
M	Tray end	¾ × 2½ × 14"	2	Pine
N	Tray bottom	¾ × 14 × 16½"	2	Plywood

Materials: Glue, 1½ × 1½" utility hinges, wood screws (#6 × 2"), knob, bullet catch, rubber bumpers, finishing materials.

Note: Measurements reflect the actual size of dimensional lumber.

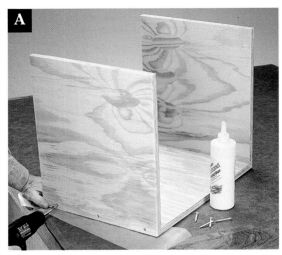

Attach the sides to the back with glue and counterbored #6 × 2" wood screws.

Drive wood screws through the back and sides to attach the shelf and divider.

Directions:
Hardware Organizer

MAKE THE CABINET. Start by cutting the sides (A), back (B) and bottom (C) to size from ¾"-thick plywood. Finish-sand the parts, and fasten the sides to the back with glue and #6 × 2" countersunk wood screws. Make sure the top and bottom edges are flush **(photo A).** Glue the bottom and fasten it to the sides and back with countersunk wood screws.

MAKE THE SHELF, DIVIDER & TOP. Cut the shelf (D), cabinet divider (E) and top (F) to size and finish-sand the parts. Center the divider from front to back on the top face of the shelf. Fasten the divider to the shelf with glue and #6 × 2" wood screws—counterbore the screw pilot holes slightly so the screw heads can be concealed with wood putty. Fasten the divider/shelf assembly to the sides and back of the cabinet, with the shelf 6" above the bottom side edges **(photo B).** Position the top onto the sides and back with a 1" overhang at the front and side edges. Attach the top to the sides, back and

Apply glue to the dowel and insert it into the hole on the top of the hardware organizer cabinet.

divider with glue and counterbored wood screws. Do not drive a screw into the center of the top panel. This area should be left open for a dowel, which will be inserted later in the assembly process.

INSERT THE DOWEL. Measure and mark points 1" back from the front top corners. Use a straightedge to draw lines from these points to the back corners of the top. The point of intersection is the center of the

project. Drill a 1"-dia. × ⅝"-deep hole at this point. Cut a 1"-dia. hardwood dowel (H) to 14" in length. Apply glue to one end of the dowel and insert it into the hole **(photo C).**

MAKE THE DOOR. Cut the door (G) to size from ¾"-thick plywood. Drill a centered, ¹¹⁄₃₂"-dia. × 1"-deep hole in the top edge of the door for the bullet catch (check the directions on the package to confirm the required dimensions

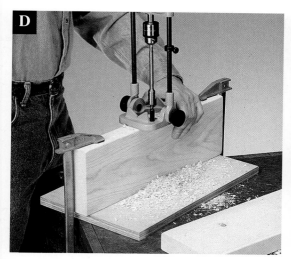

Drill a 1"-dia. hole through the handles, using a piece of scrap as a backing board.

Lay out the handle shapes separately with a straightedge, and cut them with a jig saw.

for the hole). Drill a corresponding ¼ × ¼"-dia. hole into the underside of the top. Install the bullet catch after the project has been painted. Install evenly spaced 1½" utility hinges on the door, and attach them to the bottom. Sand the entire assembly with medium-grit sandpaper to smooth out the rough edges, then install a small knob on the door.

PREPARE THE TRAY DIVIDERS. The tray dividers fit lengthwise into the trays, and feature cutouts that work as handles. The trays are sized differently, so be careful to make sure you are using the right parts for each tray. Cut the tray dividers (I) to length from 2 × 6 pine. Mark a centerpoint on the top edge of each divider. Fit a drill with a bit extender and a 1"-dia. spade bit, and drill a 1"-dia. hole all the way through the 2 × 6 at the centerpoints **(photo D).** Use a portable drill guide to ensure straight cuts. Lay out cutting lines for the handle cutouts in both dividers: mark a reference line parallel to and 1" down from each top edge. Draw a 1½"-

wide × 5"-long cutout below each reference line, centered from end to end (see *Diagram*, page 63). Make the radius cuts on each end of the handle slots with a 1½"-dia. drill bit or hole saw. Finish the handle cutout with a jig saw. Smooth out any sharp edges. Trim the top corners of the dividers to fit each tray as you assemble the trays (see sections below).

MAKE THE LARGE TRAY. Mark points on the face of one tray divider, at the ends and 3¼" up from the bottom edge. Mark points 4¼" in from each end on the top edge of the divider. Connect the points and cut along the line with a jig saw **(photo E).** Cut the large sides (J), large ends (L) and one tray bottom (N). Finish-sand all the rough edges. Center the divider on the tray bottom, and attach it with glue and counterbored wood screws, driven up through the bottom into the divider. Extend the hole in the divider through the bottom. Attach the ends to the tray bottoms with glue and screws, driven through the ends and into the tray bottom. Attach the sides

to the ends and bottom with glue and screws.

MAKE THE SMALL TRAY. Mark points on the face of the second tray divider, 1¾" up from the bottom edge. Mark points 4¼" in from each end on the top edge of the divider. Connect the points and cut along the line with a jig saw. Cut the small sides (K), small ends (M) and the other tray bottom (N), and assemble them using the same techniques used for the large tray.

APPLY FINISHING TOUCHES. Finish-sand the project, then apply primer and paint. Install the bullet catch in the door. Attach rubber bumpers or glide feet to the underside of the cabinet bottom. Insert the trays onto the dowel at the top of the cabinet.

Display Case

Even ordinary objects take on an air of importance in this decorative display case.

Vases, figurines, pottery, collectibles…everyone has something special that they'd like to show off to visitors. Whether your special item is a precious family heirloom or a unique project made by a child, exhibit it in fine fashion with this simple display case. The glass panels in the sides create a museum feeling, while protecting the contents of the case from dust and humidity. The sturdy top, while unprotected, also provides an effective display area for artwork or even potted plants.

This display case is built almost entirely from birch plywood and pine moldings. The viewing windows in the sides are simply cut out of the plywood side panels with a jig saw. Secure the glass with a frame made from corner molding around the outside of the opening, and rope-style glazier's compound and glazier's points in the inside of the opening. Corner and cove moldings are used to add a fanciful flair to the design. Bullet catches ensure that the top panel stays secure, but can still be removed easily when it's time for you to change the exhibit.

CONSTRUCTION MATERIALS

Quantity	Lumber
1	¾" × 4 × 4' birch plywood
2	1⅛ × 1⅛" × 8' pine corner molding
3	½ × ½" × 8' pine corner molding
1	⅝ × ⅝" × 6' cove molding

OVERALL SIZE:
28" HIGH
13⅝" WIDE
13⅝" LONG

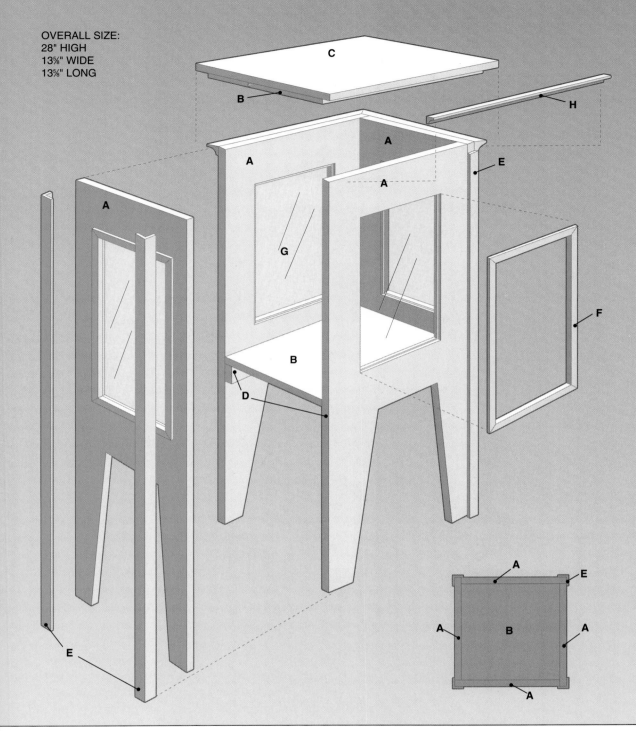

Cutting List

Key	Part	Dimension	Pcs.	Material
A	Side panel	¾ × 27¼ × 11¼"	4	Plywood
B	Shelf	¾ × 10½ × 10½"	2	Plywood
C	Top panel	¾ × 13⅝ × 13⅝"	1	Plywood
D	Cleat	¾ × 1½ × 10½"	4	Plywood

Cutting List

Key	Part	Dimension	Pcs.	Material
E	Corner trim	1⅛ × 1⅛ × 26⅝"	4	Molding
F	Window trim	½ × ½ × *	16	Molding
G	Window	⅛ × 7 × 11¼"	4	Glass
H	Cove molding	⅝ × ⅝ × 13⅜"	4	Molding

Materials: Wood glue, #6 x 1¼" wood screws, 2d finish nails, glazier's points, rope-style glazier's compound.
*Cut to fit.

Note: Measurements reflect the actual size of dimensional lumber.

Make the leg and window cutouts using a jig saw.

Fasten the shelf cleats to the side panels with wood glue and screws.

Assemble the side panels with wood glue and screws to form the display case.

Directions: Display Case

MAKE THE SIDES. The side panels are each made from one piece of plywood with tapered legs and cutouts for window openings. For uniform results, follow the instructions below to make one side, then use that side as a template for laying out the other three sides. Start by cutting the side panels (A) using a circular saw and straightedge cutting guide. Mark cutting lines for the tapered legs by drawing a line across the side panels 10" from

the bottom edge. Make marks on that line 2½" from one edge, which will be the wide edge, and 1¾" from the other, narrow edge. (The legs form square corners made with butt joints—cutting one leg of each side ¾" narrower allows for square legs that are 2½" wide in each direction.) Along the bottom edge of the side panel, make marks 1½" from the wide edge and ¾" from the narrow. Draw diagonal cutting lines connecting the marks on the inside and outside edges of each leg (see *Diagram*, page 67). Cut along the cutting lines

with a jig saw to form the tapered legs, then round over the edges of legs with medium-grit (100- to 150-grit) sandpaper. The next step is to cut the window opening. Start by drawing a line across the side panel, 2" down from the top. Draw a second line across the side panel, 13¼" down from the top. Draw perpendicular lines connecting these lines, 2½" from the edge at the wide-leg side, and 1¾" from the edge at the narrow-leg side. This will result in a rectangular cutout area that is 7" wide and 11¼" high. Drill a starter hole inside a corner of the cutout area, then cut out window opening with a jig saw. Sand all edges of the side smooth, then use it as a template to mark the legs and window openings onto the other sides. Cut out the other three sides **(photo A).**

ATTACH THE SHELF CLEATS. The shelf inside the display case is supported by shelf cleats on all four sides. Cut the cleats (D) from plywood using a circular saw and straightedge cutting guide. Attach a cleat to the inside face of each side

Mark the centers for the bullet catch receptacles on the inside surfaces of the side panels.

panel, so the top of the cleat is 1" below the window opening. One end of the cleat should be flush with the outside edge of the narrow leg. This will leave a ¾" space at the wide edge of each side panel to accept the cleat from the adjoining side. Fasten the cleats to the side panels using wood glue and #6 × 1¼" wood screws **(photo B).**

ASSEMBLE THE CASE. Apply glue to the outside edge of each narrow leg, then butt the leg against the inside face of the wide leg on the adjacent side. Drive wood screws through the wide side into the edge of the adjoining side panel. Repeat the procedure until all four side panels have been fastened **(photo C).**

INSTALL THE SHELF PANELS. Cut the two shelf panels (B) and set one aside. Sand the other shelf, then attach it to the shelf cleats with glue and wood screws—counterbore the pilot holes so the screw heads can be covered with wood putty.

MAKE & INSTALL THE TOP PANEL. Cut the top panel (C) and sand the edges smooth. Center the second shelf (B) on the underside of the top panel.

Attach it with glue and countersunk screws driven through the shelf and into the underside of the top panel. Set the top onto the top of the display case to test the fit—the shelf should fit snugly inside the frame created by the tops of the side panels. We installed bullet catches on opposite edges of the shelf to hold the top in place more securely. Drill a hole for each bullet catch in the edge of a shelf side (read the instructions on the package to find the appropriate size hole for the catches you purchase). Insert a bullet catch into each hole, then set the top back into the frame at the top of the display case. Remove the top, and check for markings from the bullet catches on the inside faces of the display case. Mark drilling points at the ends of these markings **(photo D),** then drill holes for the receptacle portions of the catches.

ATTACH THE MOLDINGS. We used pieces of corner molding and cove molding to give this display case more visual appeal. Cut strips of 1⅛" corner molding (E) the same height as the side panels, and nail them over each corner to conceal the butt joints, using 2d finish nails. Next, cut four strips of ⅝" cove molding (H) to make a frame around the top of the display case. Miter-cut the ends of the strips to make 45° miter

joints, using a power miter box or a hand miter box. Fasten the molding to the side panels with 2d finish nails. Cut the window molding (F) from corner molding. Miter-cut the corners of the frame pieces to make frames that fit inside the window openings **(photo E).**

APPLY FINISHING TOUCHES. Fill all voids and screw counterbores with wood putty, then sand all surfaces with medium (100- or 120-grit) sandpaper to smooth out rough spots. Finish-sand with fine (150- or 180-grit) sandpaper. Apply paint (we used a hard enamel paint) to all surfaces (be sure to cover the bullet catches with masking tape before painting). When the paint has dried, install the windows. Have the window glass panels (G) cut to size from ⅛"-thick glass, and insert the panels into the opening, pressed up against the edges of the corner molding frames. Press glazier's points around the perimeter of the glass panel, on the inside, using a slotted screwdriver. Press strips of rope-style glazier's compound around the inside to cover the points.

Install a frame made from corner molding around the outside edge of each window opening.

Shoe Carousel

This spinning shoe cubby puts up to 20 pairs of shoes at your beck and call in one stylish package.

Shoe storage is one of the most common household storage challenges. Whether it's because of the odd shapes of traditional foot apparel or our careless tendency to just kick them off and leave them wherever they fall at the end of a long day, shoes always seem to end up in a big, jumbled pile.

One pleasing solution to the shoe storage problem is this unique shoe carousel. Built entirely from plywood and molding, this organizer has room for up to 20 pairs of your favorite footwear. Simply rotate the entire cubby-style cabinet on the Lazy Susan turntable at the base until you locate whichever pair of high heels, flats, loafers or sneakers you are looking for.

The simple lines of this shoe carousel work well with more contemporary finishes. We chose a faux granite spray finish for the outer surfaces of the carousel, with black cubbies and base. For an added bonus, we applied 12 × 12" mirrored tiles to one side panel so you can inspect your shoes from a different perspective as you dress. The mirrors also enhance the contemporary styling.

This shoe carousel is very space efficient, occupying less than three square feet of floor space. And because it is an attractive household furnishing, you do not have to relegate it to a closet—you can display it openly in any area of your bedroom or dressing room.

CONSTRUCTION MATERIALS

Quantity	Lumber
2	½" × 4 × 8' AB plywood
1	¾" × 2 × 4' AB plywood
7	¾ × ¾" × 8' quarter-round

OVERALL SIZE:
34¾" HIGH
20" WIDE
20" LONG

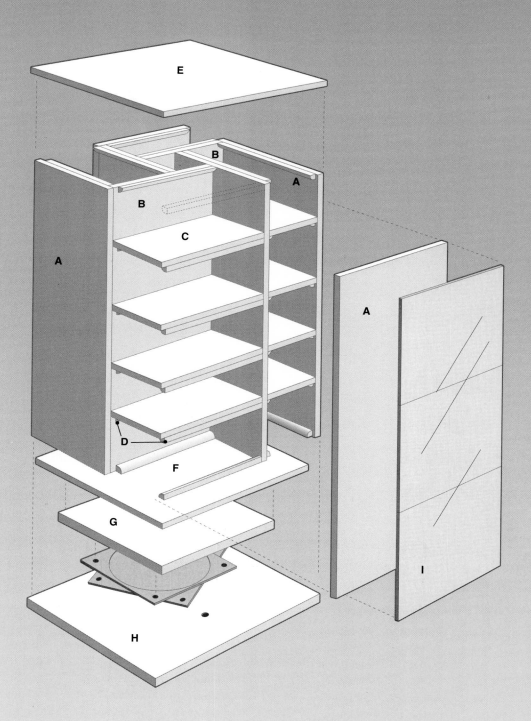

Cutting List

Key	Part	Dimension	Pcs.	Material
A	Outer panel	½ × 12½ × 32"	4	Plywood
B	Inner panel	½ × 11⅝ × 32"	4	Plywood
C	Shelf	½ × 6 × 12"	20	Plywood
D	Cleat	¾ × ¾ × 11½"	56	Molding
E	Top panel	½ × 19 × 19"	1	Plywood

Cutting List

Key	Part	Dimension	Pcs.	Material
F	Bottom	½ × 19 × 19"	1	Plywood
G	Riser	¾ × 15 × 15"	1	Plywood
H	Base	¾ × 20 × 20"	1	Plywood
I	Mirror	Cut to fit		Mirror/tile

Materials: Wood glue, #6 × 1¼" wood screws, wood putty, 6" Lazy Susan turntable, finishing materials.

Note: Measurements reflect the actual size of dimensional lumber.

Lay out cleat positions on the end and side panels and mark a ½" inset for the front edge of the cleats.

Mount the cleats to the side and end panels with wood glue and 3d finish nails.

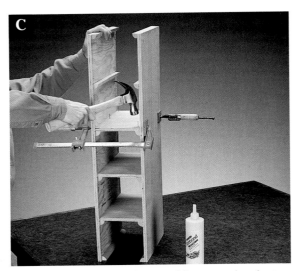

Clamp the shelves in place and fasten to the cleats.

Directions: Shoe Carousel

MAKE THE INNER & OUTER PANELS. The cabinet that forms the shoe carousel is composed of four identical racks, each with five shelves, that are fitted together in a square arrangement. The inner panel of each shelf unit fits against the back of the adjoining unit. Cut the outer panels (A) and inner panels (B) from ½"-thick plywood and sand them with medium-grit sandpaper. On the inside faces of both panels, mark the shelf cleat positions, beginning at the tops of the panels. Measure down 6½" from the top and draw a line perpendicular to the sides of the panel for the top shelf cleat (cleats also will be installed flush with the tops of the side panels). Mark the remaining cleat locations by measuring down in 6½" increments (these marks represent the tops of the cleats). The cleat for the lowest shelf (not counting the base) will be 6" above the base if you have measured correctly (see *Diagram*, page 71). Use a combination square to mark reference lines ½" in from the front and back edges of each side panel, establishing the locations for the ends of the cleats **(photo A).** Cut the cleats (D) to length from quarter-round molding. Fasten the cleats to the inner and outer panels, at the lines, using glue and 3d finish nails **(photo B).**

MAKE & INSTALL THE SHELVES. Cut the shelves (C) to size from ½"-thick plywood and sand with medium-grit sandpaper. Prop pairs of inner and outer panels upright, and position the lowest shelf on the cleats (apply glue to the tops of the cleats first). Clamp the assembly together, making sure the shelf is flush with the front and back edges of the inner (narrower) panel. Drive 3d finish nails through the edges of the shelf and into the shelf cleats. Set the nail heads with a nail set. Install the rest of the shelves **(photo C),** working your way toward the top (otherwise you won't have space to swing the hammer). Attach all the shelves in all four sections.

ATTACH THE TOP & BOTTOM. Cut the top panel (E) and bottom panel (F). Stand the shelf units upright and assemble them into a square. This may take a little trial and error, but if you've made the shelf units correctly, they should fit together easily. Refer to the *Diagram* on page 71 for a helpful view of how the units fit together. Once you have the puzzle solved, bind the shelf units together with heavy tape to keep them in place **(photo D).** Place the top panel rough side down on the shelf unit so all edges are flush. Fasten the top panel to the shelf units and top cleats with glue and 3d finish nails. Turn the assembly upside down and fasten the bottom panel in the same manner. Remove the tape.

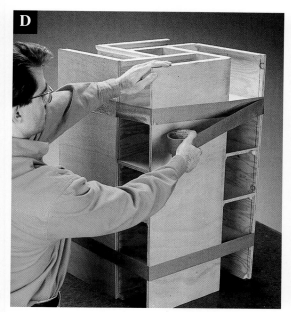

Stand the shelf units up and wrap them together with duct tape to hold them in place for assembly.

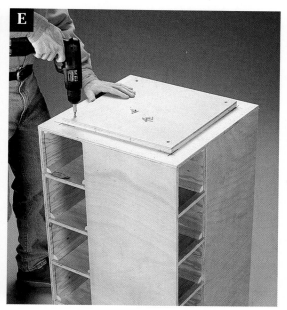

Fasten the riser to the bottom panel using wood glue and 1¼" wood screws.

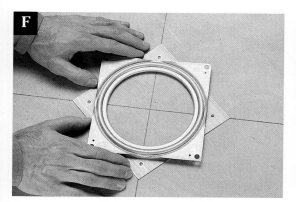

Align mounting holes in the Lazy Susan with diagonals lines drawn on the base.

Drive screws through the access hole in the base to attach the Lazy Susan to the riser.

ATTACH THE RISER & BASE. The riser is essentially a spacer that fits between the bottom panel of the cabinet and the carousel space to create enough clearance for the cabinet to spin easily. Cut the riser (G) and base (H). Center the riser on the bottom panel, and fasten it with glue and 1¼" wood screws **(photo E).** Draw diagonal lines on the riser and the base, connecting opposite corners, to use as a reference for attaching the Lazy Susan turntable. Position the Lazy Susan so the mounting holes are aligned with the reference lines on the base **(photo F),** and attach the Lazy Susan using the screws provided with the hardware. Once the Lazy Susan is attached, rotate it ¼ turn and mark a point onto the base through one of the mounting holes. Drill a 1"-dia. access hole through the base at this point. Set the Lazy Susan and base onto the riser, and look through the access hole to make sure the free mounting plate is aligned with the reference lines on the riser. Once it is in position, spin the base so the access hole is centered over the screw locations, and drive screws to attach the Lazy Susan to the riser **(photo G).**

APPLY FINISHING TOUCHES. Fill all counterbores and exposed plywood edges with wood putty, then sand all the surfaces. Apply the finish—we spray-painted the base and the insides of the cubbies black, then masked them off and sprayed faux granite paint onto the sides and top of the cabinet. We also attached 12 × 12" mirrored tiles to one side.

Paint Center

Keep your painting equipment and supplies in one convenient location with this paint center.

Painting supplies have an amazing ability to create a mess in your basement or garage. Half-full paint cans, crusty brushes and sleeves, stirring sticks, drop cloths, roller trays, cans of solvent and cleaners…the tools and supplies used in painting seem to multiply every time you start a new project, and if they are left unchecked they will take over your work spaces in a hurry.

The solution? An efficient paint center that lets you store all your equipment and supplies in one spot.

The paint center shown here is composed of two main elements: a work area where you can mix the paint and clean up brushes and other equipment; and a roomy can rack that is designed specifically for paint can storage.

The main worksurface on this paint center contains a square cutout that allows you to wipe up spills easily, and is sized to frame a standard dishpan (set it on the shelf below) for cleaning up brushes and roller sleeves. The broad storage areas below the worksurface are spacious enough to hold drop cloths, roller trays, and oversized paint or solvent containers. The can rack at the side of the work area is sized to hold 1-gallon paint cans efficiently —no more stacking cans or searching for the right supplies every time you start a project. Drying rods for rags and a pegboard back panel for hanging paint brushes are bonus features that you will find very handy.

CONSTRUCTION MATERIALS

Quantity	Lumber
6	2 × 4" × 8' pine
4	1 × 10" × 8' pine
2	1 × 2" × 8' pine
1	¾" × 4' × 8' plywood
2	⅛" × 4' × 8' pegboard
1	½" × 10' quarter-round molding

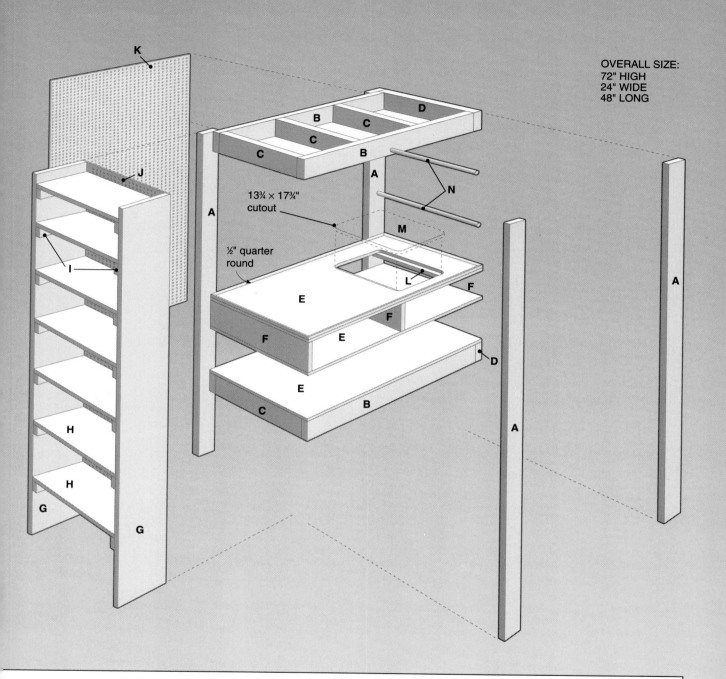

OVERALL SIZE:
72" HIGH
24" WIDE
48" LONG

K

J

13¾ × 17¾"
cutout

½" quarter
round

A

A

B

C

C

C

B

C

B

D

A

N

M

L

E

E

F

F

F

F

E

D

E

B

C

A

I

I

H

H

G

G

G

Cutting List

Key	Part	Dimension	Pcs.	Material
A	Post	1½ × 3½ × 72"	4	Pine
B	Cross rail	1½ × 3½ × 35½"	4	Pine
C	Short rail	1½ × 3½ × 21"	4	Pine
D	End rail	1½ × 3½ × 24"	2	Pine
E	Work area shelf	¾ × 24 × 36¾"	3	Plywood
F	Divider	¾ × 7 × 24"	3	Plywood
G	Can shelf side	¾ × 9¼ × 72"	2	Pine

Cutting List

Key	Part	Dimension	Pcs.	Material
H	Can shelf	¾ × 9¼ × 22½"	7	Pine
I	Shelf cleat	¾ × 1½ × 9¼"	14	Pine
J	Can shelf back	⅛ × 24 × 72"	1	Pegboard
K	Work area back	⅛ × 31½ × 72"	1	Pegboard
L	Cover cleat	¾ × 2 × 16"	2	Plywood
M	Cutout cover	¾ × 13¾ × 17¾"	1	Plywood
N	Drying rod	1"-dia. × 24"	2	Dowel

Materials: Glue, wood screws (#6 × 1¼", #6 × 2", #6 × 2½"), 1" wire brads, finishing materials.

Note: Measurements reflect the actual size of dimensional lumber.

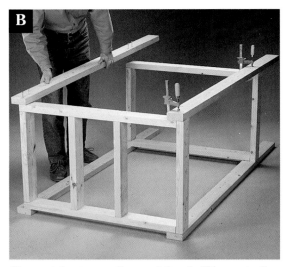

Complete the top section of the work area frame by attaching the end rail to the ends of the cross rails with #6 × 2½" wood screws.

Connect the top section and the shelf frame to the posts to assemble the work area frame.

The 2 × 4 framework for the work area section is the backbone of the paint center. Smooth out any sharp edges after it is assembled.

Directions: Paint Center

BUILD THE WORK AREA FRAMEWORK. The work area of the paint center is supported by a four-post 2 × 4 framework with a top section and a shelf support frame. The top section and the shelf support frame fit between the posts to give the framework its structure and keep it in square. The top section and the shelf frame are nearly identical 2 × 4 frames—the main difference is that the top section contains two short rails in the center for extra strength. Start by cutting the 2 × 4 cross rails (B), short rails (C) and end rails (D). Sandwich a short rail between each pair of cross rails, at one end only. Attach the short rails between the cross rails with glue and countersunk #6 × 2½" screws driven through the cross rails and into the ends of the short rails. Select one assembly to use for the top section, and install a pair of evenly spaced short rails between the cross

Drill a 1"-dia. starter hole at the front inside corner, then make the worksurface cutout with a jig saw.

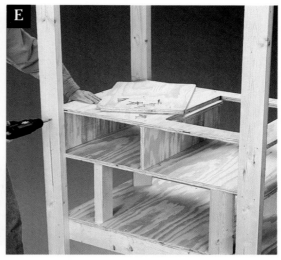

Install the lower work area shelf first. Use 2 × 4 spacers to support the middle shelf while you work.

rails (about 12" from the ends of the cross rails). Attach an end rail to the ends of each cross rail pair with glue and screws driven through the end rail and into the cross rails **(photo A).** Cut the 2 × 4" posts (A), and arrange them around the outside corners of the top section and the shelf support frame. The top section should be flush with the post tops, and the bottom of the shelf support frame should be 16½" up from the post bottoms. Adjust the parts so the posts overhang the frames by 1¾" on one side to create a recess for the can shelf to fit between the posts. Clamp the parts together with bar clamps or C-clamps **(photo B).** Check to make sure the assembly is square, then fasten the parts together with glue and screws driven through the posts and into the top section and frame. To make assembly easier, start the screws in the offset posts before squaring everything up. Stand the assembly upright and smooth out any sharp edges with a sander **(photo C).**

Make the work area shelves. The work area has three shelves that are identical in size. The top shelf serves as a worksurface, and features a square cutout on the right side. The middle shelf and lower shelf are separated by dividers. They create storage and a resting place so a dishpan can be set below the cutout in the worksurface. The worksurface and middle shelf are attached with screws driven through the posts. The lower shelf rests on the shelf support frame of the work area framework. Start by cutting the work area shelves (E) to size from ¾"-thick plywood. Mark a 13¾ × 17¾" cutout 4½" from the right edge of one shelf, centered front to back. Use a 1"-dia. spade bit to drill a starter hole at the front, inside corner of the cutout. Use the hole as a starter for the jig saw blade as you cut out the rectangle **(photo D).** Cut carefully and save the waste to use for the cover for the cutout (M). The 1"-dia. hole will form a finger grip for removing the cover. Sand the edges of the cover and the cutout smooth.

Install the work area shelves. Install the lower shelf first by setting it on the shelf support frame and attaching with glue and screws. Cut four pieces of 2 × 4 to 11¾" in length to use as spacers, and set them on end on the lower shelf. Set the middle shelf onto the spacers, and drive counterbored screws through the posts and into the edges of the shelf. Drive two screws at each joint. Cut the dividers (F) and cover cleats (L) to size from plywood. Fasten the cleats to the underside of the worksurface shelf to create a 1" ledge inside the cutout (the ledge will support the cutout cover). Set the dividers on the middle shelf— one should be between the offset posts, flush with the edge of the shelf, and the other should be 20" in from the right edge of the shelf, flush with the front edge. Attach the dividers to the middle shelf with glue and screws driven up through the underside of the middle shelf and into the bottom edges of the dividers. Set the worksurface shelf on the top edges of the dividers, and drive screws through the posts and into the edges of the dividers and the worksurface shelf **(photo E).**

INSTALL THE WORK AREA BACK. Cut the work area back (K) to size from ⅛"-thick pegboard. Fasten the work area back to the back edges of the shelves and to the posts with #6 × 1¼" screws, making sure the work area frame is still square.

BUILD THE CAN SHELF. The can shelf part of the paint center is a cabinet-style shelf system with a pegboard back and plywood sides. It is designed to fit between the offset posts on the left side of the work area. Start building it by cutting the can shelf sides (G), can shelves (H) and the shelf cleats (I). Lay the shelf sides next to one another, with their tops and bottoms flush. Mark layout lines for the shelf locations onto the inside faces of the shelf sides, at 9¼" intervals,

The can shelf unit should fit snugly between the offset posts on the left side of the work area.

starting at the bottom. Marking both sides at the same time ensures that the shelves will be properly aligned. Attach shelf cleats to the shelf sides, butted up against the layout lines and flush with the back and front edges of the side panels. Use glue and two #6 × 1¼" screws to attach each cleat. Drill two pilot holes through the shelf sides, ⅜" above the top of each cleat. Set the shelf sides upright, with the inside faces facing one another, and install shelves that rest on the top cleats and the bottom cleats. Before installing the rest of the can shelves, test-fit the assembly in the recess between the posts on the left edge of the work area **(photo F).** If the

shelf assembly is too wide, you will need to remove the top and bottom shelves, then trim all the shelves to fit. Fasten the rest of the can shelves, resting on the cleats, with glue and screws. Next, cut the can shelf back (J) from ⅛" pegboard, and attach it to the backs of the shelves and the shelf sides with glue and #6 × 1¼" screws.

INSTALL THE CAN SHELF. Set the can shelf assembly between the offset posts on the left side of the work area. Attach the shelf to the posts by driving #6 × 2" wood screws through the shelf sides and into the shelf posts **(photo G).**

Attach the can shelf unit between the posts with glue and #6 × 2" screws driven through the shelf sides into the posts.

Use 1" wire brads to secure a quarter-round molding frame around the edges of the worksurface.

FRAME THE WORKSURFACE. We designed this paint center with a frame made from trim molding tacked around the perimeter of the worksurface. The frame helps contain small paint spills so the paint does not run off the surface and onto the floor. We used ½" quarter-round molding to make the frame. To frame the work-surface, use a miter box (power or hand operated) to make a 45° miter cut at the end of a piece of quarter-round molding and set it on the back edge of the worksurface. The outside corner of the cut end should be flush with the edges of the worksurface. Make a mark onto the molding at the opposite end of the worksur-face, and cut another 45° miter cut that points in the opposite direction of the first cut. Attach the piece of molding to the back of the worksurface with 1" wire brads. Butt the mitered end of the molding piece next to the molding you have in-stalled, so the two make a square corner. Mark a cutting line on the quarter-round piece, and miter-cut to fit. Con-tinue cutting the remaining two pieces of the frame in this fash-ion, then install them with glue and wire brads to complete the worksurface frame **(photo H).**

APPLY FINISHING TOUCHES. Add a towel and rag drying rack to the paint center by drilling 1"-dia. holes through the front and back posts on the right side of the work area—we positioned the holes 12½" and 21½" from the post tops. Cut 1"-dia. dowels to 24" in length to make the drying rods (N). Apply glue to the surfaces of the 1" guide holes, and insert the rods so the ends are flush with the outside edges of the front and back posts. Sand the dowel ends smooth, if necessary, after the glue has dried. Also give all the wood sur-faces a light finish sanding before apply-ing your finish of choice. We applied clear polyurethane di-rectly to the unstained, unpainted wood to create a surface that is easy to clean.

TIP

Use special pegboard hooks to hang items from pegboard. Sold at any hardware store or building center, the hooks can be moved from hole to hole easily, with-out stripping out pegboard holes (as screws will).

Sewing Chest

*Soft lines, a spacious interior and a removable tray make this chest
a perfect companion for sewing, knitting or needlepoint hobbyists.*

CONSTRUCTION MATERIALS

Quantity	Lumber
1	¾" × 4' × 8' plywood
1	¼" × 4' × 4' plywood
1	½ × 2¼" × 8' beaded molding

With this clever sewing chest, you can move from room to room in pursuit of your crafting hobby, without leaving a trail of tools and materials in your wake. The padded lid flips up for access to a removable tray and the generous storage compartment below. The up-holstered top can be used as a footrest, a seat, or even a temporary pincushion—just be careful not to mix the uses. This sewing chest is designed to be the perfect size for most sewing, knitting and fabric art projects. It's big enough to hold all your tools and supplies, but still lightweight and portable.

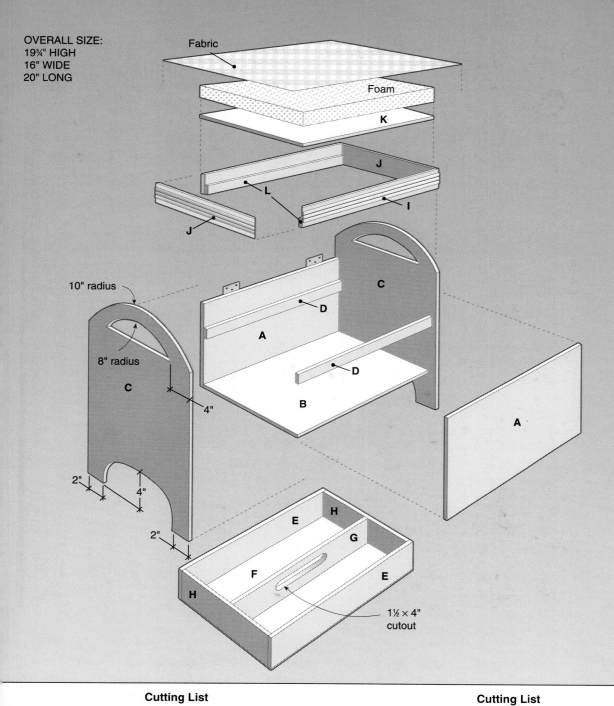

OVERALL SIZE:
19¾" HIGH
16" WIDE
20" LONG

Fabric

Foam

K

J

L

I

J

10" radius

8" radius

C

4"

D

A

D

B

C

2"

4"

2"

E

H

G

F

E

H

A

1½ × 4"
cutout

Key	Part	Dimension	Pcs.	Material
A	Front/back	¾ × 9¾ × 18½"	2	Plywood
B	Bottom	¾ × 14 × 18½"	1	Plywood
C	Chest end	¾ × 16 × 20"	2	Plywood
D	Tray cleat	¾ × 1½ × 18¼"	2	Plywood
E	Tray side	¾ × 3 × 18"	2	Plywood
F	Tray bottom	¼ × 13¾ × 18"	1	Plywood

Cutting List

Key	Part	Dimension	Pcs.	Material
G	Tray divider	¾ × 3 × 16½"	1	Plywood
H	Tray end	¾ × 3 × 12¼"	2	Plywood
I	Side molding	½ × 2¼ × 18¼"	2	Molding
J	End molding	½ × 2¼ × 15½"	2	Molding
K	Seatboard	¾ × 14⅜ × 17⅛"	1	Plywood
L	Seat cleat	¾ × 1 × 17¼"	2	Plywood

Cutting List

Materials: Glue, wood screws (#6 × 1¼", #6 × 2"), 4d finish nails, 1" wire brads, 1"-thick foam, upholstery fabric, 1½ × 1¼" butt hinges, finishing materials.

Specialty Items: 1½"-dia. hole saw, scissors.

Note: Measurements reflect the actual size of dimensional lumber.

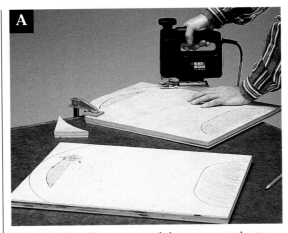

Make the handle cutout and the curves at the top and bottom of the end panels with a jig saw.

Make the ends of the handle cutout in the divider with a hole saw, then connect with a jig saw.

Directions: Sewing Chest

CUT THE CHEST ENDS. The ends of the sewing chest have curved tops and bottoms, and handle cutouts that are made with a jig saw. Start by cutting the ends (C) to size from ¾"-thick plywood. Use a straight-edge to draw a centerline from top to bottom on each side (to use as a reference for drawing the curved cutting lines). To draw cutting lines for the top curves, tack a finishing nail into each end panel, 10" down from the top on the centerline. Tie a string to the nail, and measure out 10" on the string. Tie a pencil at this point. With the string taut, draw a curve from side to side of the end panel. To draw cutting lines for the handle cutouts, adjust the pencil so it is 8" from the nail, and draw a semicircle below the top cutting arc. Connect the points where the 10" curve meets the sides of each end panel to create the straight bottom of the handle cutouts. To make the bottom cutting lines, mark points 2" in from each side of each end panel, at the bottoms. Mark another point 4" up from the bottom of each panel, on the centerline. Draw an 8"-long line at the 4" mark, parallel to the bottom of each end panel. Connect the end-points of these lines with a smooth arc to the 2" points. Cut the top and bottom curves with a jig saw **(photo A),** and sand

After making the handle cutout in the divider, attach it between the tray ends with glue and finish nails.

smooth with a drum sander attachment on your power drill. Drill starter holes, then make the handle cutouts with a jig saw. Sand the handle cutouts smooth with a thin metal sanding block.

ASSEMBLE THE CHEST. Cut the front and back panels (A), the bottom (B), and the tray cleats (D). Attach the cleats to the inside faces of the front and back panels so the tops of the cleats are 6½" above the bottoms of the panels. Use glue and #6 × 1¼" wood screws. Attach the bottom between the front and back panels with glue and #6 × 2" screws, making sure the ends of the pieces are flush. Install the assembly between the end panels: the underside of the bottom should be flush with the tops of the cutouts on the bottoms of the end panels, and the front and back should each be recessed ¼" from the sides of the end panels. Use glue and #6 × 2" counterbored screws driven through the outside faces of the end panels and into the front, back and bottom. Cut the tray sides (E), tray bottom (F), tray divider (G), and tray ends (H). Mark a centerpoint on one face

After stapling or tacking the upholstery material over the foam-rubber padding, trim off the excess material with scissors.

Sandwich knitting needles or other light items between strips of Velcro® attached to the underside of the seat. Cover the backs of the outer strips with upholstery for a decorative look.

of the divider. Draw a 4"-long line through the centerpoint, parallel to the top and bottom of the divider. Mark points on the line 1¼" on each side of the centerpoint. Install a 1½"-dia. hole saw on your portable drill and drill holes at these points. Connect the holes with a jig saw, then sand smooth with a drum sander attachment to create the handle cutout in the divider **(photo B).** Fasten the tray sides to the tray ends with glue and 4d finish nails. Attach the tray bottom in the same way. Attach the divider between the ends **(photo C).** Use a nail set to set all exposed nail heads.

BUILD THE SEAT. The sewing chest seat is composed of pieces of 2¼"-wide beaded molding that frame a plywood seatboard. The seatboard is padded with 1"-thick foam rubber and covered with upholstery material. Start by cutting the beaded molding to make the sides and ends (I, J) of the seat frame. Use a power miter box or a hand miter box and backsaw to cut 45° miters at

the ends of each frame piece so the pieces fit together to form a square frame. Assemble the frame using glue and 1" wire brads driven through pilot holes at each joint. If you own a picture frame clamp, this is an excellent time to use it. Otherwise, clamp the frame from both directions with bar or pipe clamps, checking to make sure the corners are square. Cut the seat cleats (L) and seatboard (K) to size. Attach the cleats to the sides of the seat frame (after the glue has dried), flush with the bottom edges, using glue and 4d finish nails. Fill plywood edges with putty, finish-sand, and paint the chest before proceeding.

MAKE THE SEAT CUSHION. Cut a piece of 1"-thick foam rubber the same size as the seatboard. Cut a piece of upholstery material large enough to cover the foam and the seatboard, overhanging by at least 4" on each side. Fold the upholstery over the foam and seat board, and tack or staple it along the edges **(photo D).** Set the seat onto the seat cleats in the seat frame, and attach by

driving 4d finish nails through the frame and into the seat board. For a handy touch, cut self-adhesive Velcro® strips and stick them to the underside of the seat. Stick a piece of upholstery fabric to the matching part of each strip **(photo E).** Use the strips to secure knitting needles or other light crafting items. Finally, attach the seat to the chest with 1½ × 1¼" butt hinges **(photo F).**

Attach the seat to the back of the chest with two evenly spaced 1½ × 1¼" butt hinges.

Guest Towel Caddy

When your good friends arrive, just pull this welcoming, pineapple-shaped caddy out of the closet and put it in the guest bedroom— keeping them stocked up with all their bathroom articles.

PROJECT
POWER TOOLS

When guests come to stay, this towel caddy makes it easy to keep their bedroom stocked. Designed as a portable storage unit, a fully stocked guest towel caddy is easily stored in a linen closet. When the honored guests arrive, what could be more welcoming than a pineapple-shaped towel caddy in their room? After all, the pineapple is a traditional welcome motif. In addition to keeping your friends in clean towels and toiletries, this project adds a quaint decorative touch to any guest bedroom. Just roll your towels and store them in the easy-to-build cubbies, which are open-ended on the front and closed at the back. Two shelves are positioned across the top for bathroom amenities like soap bars or scrub pads. A dowel handle is inserted along the top of the linen organizer to make the entire unit easy to move from room to room.

Making the linen organizer is a simple process. We started with the cubbies, which are assembled with rectangular pine boards, glued and screwed together in simple butt joints. Draw a grid with 1" squares on a plywood workpiece, and transfer the design from the *Diagram* on page 85. After the front and back standards have been cut to shape and painted, it's just a matter of positioning the shelves in between them and fastening them with 4d finish nails and wood screws, completing the project.

CONSTRUCTION MATERIALS

Quantity	Lumber
2	1 × 10" × 8' pine
1	¾" × 4' × 4' plywood
1	¾"-dia. × 3' dowel
1	¾ × ¾" × 4' quarter round
1	³⁄₁₆ × ¾" × 6' nosing

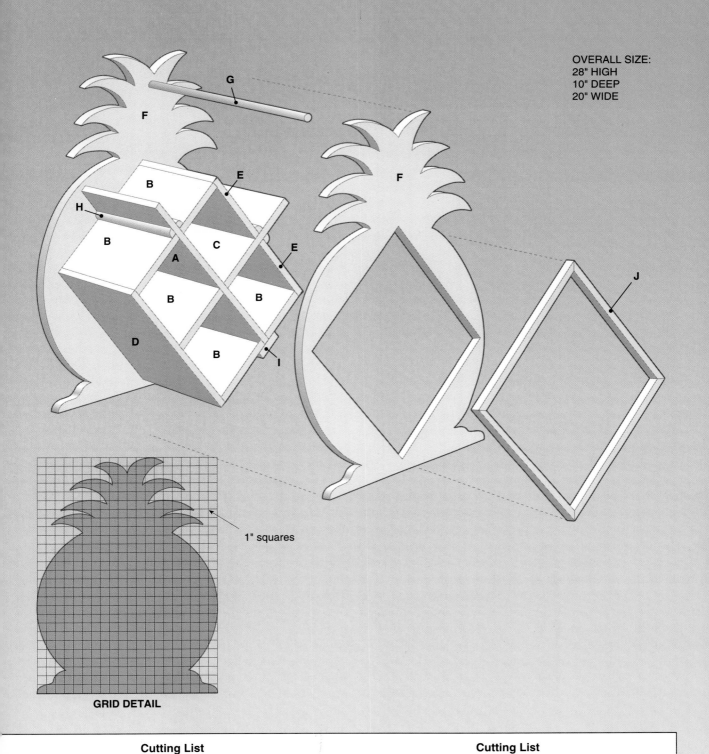

OVERALL SIZE:
28" HIGH
10" DEEP
20" WIDE

1" squares

GRID DETAIL

Cutting List

Key	Part	Dimension	Pcs.	Material
A	Cubby shelf	¾ × 9¼ × 16½"	1	Pine
B	Cubby divider	¾ × 9¼ × 5½"	5	Pine
C	Cubby center	¾ × 9¼ × 9½"	1	Pine
D	Cubby base	¾ × 9¼ × 13¼"	1	Pine
E	Cubby top	¾ × 9¼ × 6¼"	2	Pine

Cutting List

Key	Part	Dimension	Pcs.	Material
F	Standard	¾ × 20 × 28"	2	Plywood
G	Handle	¾ × 10"	1	Dowel
H	Corner brace	¾ × ¾ × 8½"	4	Pine
I	Cleat	¾ × 3 × 9¼"	1	Pine
J	Shelf nosing	3⁄16 × ¾ × 14"	4	Molding

Materials: Glue, wood screws (#6 × 1¼", #6 × 2"), 4d finish nails, 1¼" brads, finishing materials.

Note: Measurements reflect the actual size of dimensional lumber.

Use a jig saw to cut a notch in one corner of the cubby center and cubby shelf.

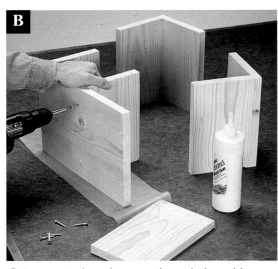

Drive counterbored screws through the cubby base into the cubby dividers.

Attach a cubby divider and cubby top to the cubby shelf with glue and counterbored wood screws.

Directions:
Guest Towel Caddy

MAKE THE CUBBY PARTS. The storage cubbies for the guest towels are formed by a frame that is divided into four equal-sized quadrants. The frame and cubbies are made up of ten boards that are glued and screwed together—pay close attention to the assembly order. Basically the frame and cubbies are created in two halves that are joined together with a long board, the cubby shelf, in between. Cut the cubby shelf (A), cubby dividers (B), cubby center (C), cubby base (D) and cubby tops (E) to size. Sand the pieces with medium (100- or 120-grit) sandpaper to smooth out the rough spots, then use a jig saw to cut a ¾"-deep × 3¼"-long notch along one corner of the cubby shelf and cubby center **(photo A).** Cut the notches so they run down the long edge of the parts. These notches allow you to fit the front standard over the finished cubby assembly.

ASSEMBLE THE CUBBIES. The first step in assembling the cubbies is to attach the corner braces (H) to the cubby center and cubby shelf. Start by cutting the corner braces to length from quarter-round molding with a jig saw. Attach them across the width of the cubby center and cubby shelf so that the flat side of each corner brace is flush with the short edge of each notch. Attach a strip along both faces of each cubby shelf and the cubby center. Use glue and finish nails to attach the corner braces. Before attaching the cubby center to the cubby shelf, you must mark the relative position of the parts. Use a straightedge to measure and mark a line across the width of the cubby shelf, 6¼" from the bottom edge (the short edge opposite from the notch). Mark a second line across the width, ¾" above the first. Apply glue to the bottom edge of the cubby center, and attach it to the cubby shelf between the guidelines with counterbored, #6 × 1¼" wood screws. Next, fasten the cubby

Trace the shelf outline on the front, creating guidelines for the cutout.

dividers to one end of each cubby top with glue and counterbored wood screws driven through the cubby tops into the dividers. Make sure the edges are flush. Attach a cubby divider at both ends of the cubby base and at its center, forming the bottom cap assembly **(photo B).** Make sure the edges are flush. Use glue and counterbored wood screws to attach the cubby dividers and their cubby tops to the cubby shelf on each side of the cubby center **(photo C).** Drive the screws through the cubby shelf to hold the cubby dividers. Drive brads through the corner braces into the cubby tops. Attach the cubby base and its cubby dividers to the cubby shelf with glue. Drive brads through the corner braces into the cubby dividers on the cubby base. Cut the cleat (I) to size, and center it on the bottom edge of the cubby shelf. Attach it lengthwise to the cubby dividers and the cubby shelf edge with glue and counterbored wood screws. The cleat strengthens the construc-

tion. Clamp the cubby assembly and let it dry.

CUT OUT THE STANDARDS. The standards are the large, decorative faces on the front and back of the caddy. To make the standards (F), you must transfer the pattern in the *Diagram* on page 85. Lay out a grid with 1" squares on your plywood parts, and use the standard pattern as a reference for drawing the shape. Cut out the design with a jig saw, and smooth out the rough edges with medium-grit sandpaper.

MAKE THE CUBBY CUTOUT. Center the cubbies on one standard so the bottom corner is ½" above the standard's bottom edge. Trace around the cubbies **(photo D).** Remove the cubbies and redraw the lines with a straightedge, ignoring the outlines of the quarter-round molding strips. Cut along the square outline with a jig saw and a straightedge guide. Place the front standard over the rear standard, and trace the cutout outline.

ATTACH THE CUBBIES & STANDARDS. Drill pilot holes for wood screws every 4" along the

cubby assembly's back edges. Make sure the pilot holes are centered in the edges. Measure and mark 24⅜" from the bottom of the standards. Drill centered, ¾"-dia. holes at these points for the dowel handle. Stand the front standard upright, and slide the cubbies into the front cutout so that the edges are flush. Slide a ½"-thick piece of scrap beneath the cubbies for support. Drive 4d finish nails through the cubbies into the standard, and through the standard into the cubby shelf and cubby center **(photo E).** To secure the back standard, drive screws through the back into the cubbies.

APPLY FINISHING TOUCHES. Cut the handle (G) to length. Apply glue to the handle ends, and slide the handle into place. Miter-cut the shelf nosing (J) to fit around the shelves on the front. Attach the shelf nosing around the cutout with glue and 1" wire brads. Set the nails and fill the nail holes. Finish-sand the guest towel caddy. Prime the surfaces, and finish them with a latex paint.

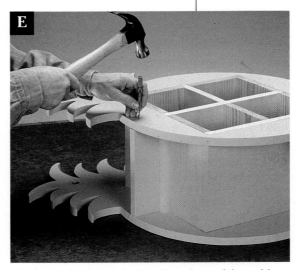

Attach the front standard to the edges of the cubby with finish nails and glue.

Under-bed Storage Box

*Put wasted space beneath a bed to work
with this simple roll-out storage box.*

Even a standard twin-size bed conceals 15 cubic feet or more of storage space beneath the box spring. Instead of letting that valuable space become simply a gathering spot for dust bunnies, put it to good use with this under-bed storage box. Generously proportioned and designed to roll in and out effortlessly from under your bed, it is a perfect spot to store off-season clothing, bulky sweaters, or even special mementos. And because the sliding compartment lids are made of aromatic cedar, your cherished fabric items will be safe from moths and other pests.

Construction of the under-bed storage box is very simple. It is basically a pine frame with a center divider and cleats for the lids and the bottom panels. We mounted bed-box rollers at all four corners so the box can slide in and out easily. Bed-box rollers are specialty hardware

items that can be purchased at most hardware stores or woodworker's stores. Because they are hard plastic, they will not damage or discolor carpeting.

The pine, plywood and cedar used in the under-bed storage box make it suitable for just about any type of finish. Because it spends most of its time under the bed, you may prefer not to spend a lot of time and effort creating a beautiful finish. But you should at least seal the pine and plywood with a clear topcoat for protection. We painted the box as well to give it a little more appeal. Do not apply a finish to the aromatic cedar if you want it to retain its fragrance.

CONSTRUCTION MATERIALS

Quantity	Lumber
3	1 × 2" × 8' pine
2	1 × 3" × 8' pine
2	1 × 6" × 8' pine
1	⅜" × 4 × 8' BC plywood
1	¼" × 4 × 8' aromatic cedar

OVERALL SIZE:
5½" HIGH
30" WIDE
60" LONG

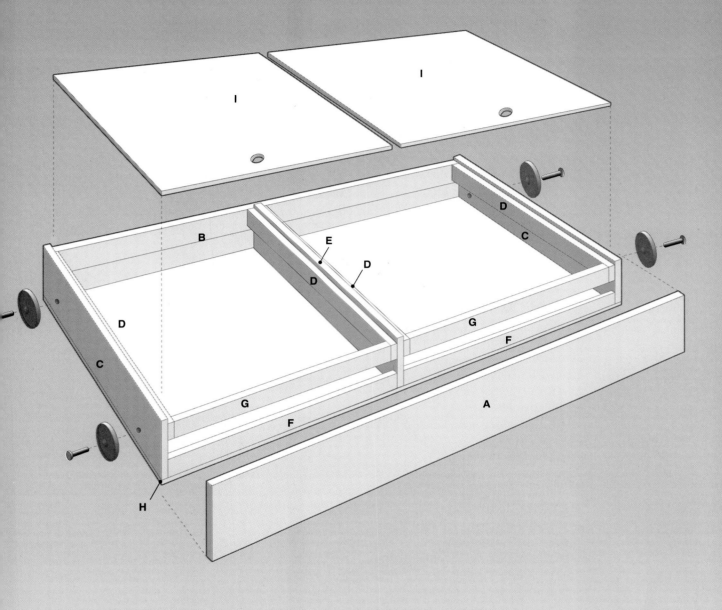

Cutting List

Key	Part	Dimension	Pcs.	Material
A	Box front	¾ × 5½ × 60"	1	Pine
B	Box back	¾ × 2½ × 56½"	2	Pine
C	Box side	¾ × 5½ × 29¼"	2	Pine
D	Lid support	¾ × 1½ × 28½"	4	Pine
E	Divider	¾ × 5½ × 28½"	1	Pine

Cutting List

Key	Part	Dimension	Pcs.	Material
F	Bottom cleat	¾ × 1½ × 27¾"	2	Pine
G	Top cleat	¾ × 1½ × 26¼"	2	Pine
H	Bottom panel	⅜ × 29¼ × 58"	1	Plywood
I	Sliding lid	¼ × 27¾ × 29¼"	2	Aromatic cedar

Materials: Bed-box rollers w/mounting bolts, #6 × 1¼" and #6 × 2" wood screws, wood glue.

Note: Measurements reflect the actual size of dimensional lumber.

Directions:
Under-bed Storage Box

MAKE THE FRAME. The frame for the under-bed storage box is a basic box made with butt joints. The front board on the box overhangs the sides by 1" to conceal the front bed-box rollers that are mounted to the sides. Cut the box front (A) and box sides (C) to size from 1 × 6 pine, and cut the box back (B) parts from 1 × 3 pine (when laid edge to edge, two 1 × 3s are ½" shorter than one 1 × 6, which will create a recess for mounting the bottom panel). Sand all parts smooth. Draw a reference line on the inside face of the box front, 1" in from each side. Set the box front on a spacer made from ½" plywood. Align the box sides at the inside edges of the reference lines (check to make sure the top of the box front is ⁵⁄₁₆" higher than the tops of the side), and attach them to the front with glue and #6 × 2" wood screws—counterbore the screws so the heads can be covered with wood putty. Attach one of the box back 1 × 3s between the sides, flush with the bottom edges, using glue and screws. Attach the other 1 × 3 between the sides, making sure the edges of the two back parts are butted together

Fasten the back between the sides using wood glue and counterbored screws. Use wood spacer blocks to keep bottom edges flush.

Clamp the lid supports in position flush with the tops of the box front and back, then fasten them with wood glue and screws.

tightly, and there is a ½" gap between the top of the back and the sides **(photo A).**

INSTALL THE FRAME DIVIDER & CLEATS. Mark centerpoints on the inside faces of the box front and box backs: the front centerpoint is 30" from the ends; the back centerpoint is 28¼" from the ends (measure from the ends of the back, not the outside faces of the box). Cut the divider (E), then position it between the front and back of the box, with the end of the divider centered on the centerpoints. The top of the divider should be

⁵⁄₁₆" above the tops of the front and back. Attach the divider with glue and screws driven through the front and back and into the ends of the divider. Cut the lid supports (D), top cleats (G), and bottom cleats (F). Attach the lid supports to the sides of the divider, flush with the tops of the front and back. Use glue and #6 × 1¼" wood screws **(photo B).** Attach the bottom cleats to the inside face of the box front, flush with the bottom edges of the sides. Position the top cleats between the lid supports, against the inside face of

If the top and bottom cleats are too long, mark them against the opening for trimming.

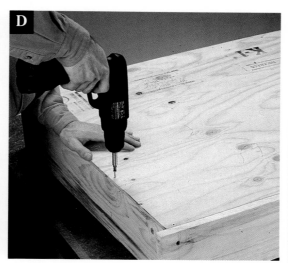

Cut the bottom panel to size, then fasten it to the bottom edges of the box frame and divider.

Mount bed-box rollers on the outside faces of the sides so the rollers extend ½" below the box bottom.

the box front. If the cleats are too long, mark them for trimming to length **(photo C).** Attach the top cleats to the inside face of the box front, flush with the tops of the lid supports.

ATTACH THE BOTTOM PANEL. Cut the bottom panel (H) to size from ⅜" plywood. Turn the frame assembly upside down and apply glue to the bottom edges of the frame components. Fasten the bottom panel to the frame assembly by driving screws through the bottom into the edges of the frame and the divider **(photo D).**

INSTALL THE SLIDING LIDS. Cut the sliding lids (I) to size from ¼"-thick aromatic cedar pressboard. Mark centerpoints (13⅞" from the sides) 2" in from the front edge of each lid. Drill 1"-dia. holes through the centerpoints to create finger grips for sliding the lids back and forth. Sand all edges of the lids, as well as the finger-grip cutouts, to prevent splinters when handling the lids. The lids are designed to simply rest on the lid supports between the divider and the sides of the frame. Because they are not

attached permanently, they can be lifted off for easy access, in addition to sliding back and forth on the lid supports. If you are using the under-bed storage box in a spot where it may be kicked or jostled frequently, you can hold the lids in place more securely by driving finish nails into the inside faces of the sides and dividers, just above the lid.

APPLY THE FINISHING TOUCHES. Fill all counterbored screw holes with wood putty, then sand the entire unit with fine (120- to 150-grit) sandpaper. Install the bed-box rollers on the outside faces of the sides, 3" in from the front and the back. The rollers should extend ½" below the bottom edges of the sides **(photo E).** Remove the rollers and axles for finishing. We painted the storage box, then topcoated it with polyurethane (except for the cedar lids, which were left unfinished). Reinstall the rollers and mount chest handles or straps (optional) on the front to make the box easier to slide in and out from under the bed.

Family Bike Rack

Store two adult-size bikes and two children's bikes in this efficient rack. Or, if you are a serious cyclist, you can store four full-size bikes by making one simple modification to the design.

PROJECT
POWER TOOLS

Bicycles are a convenient and efficient means of transportation, but finding a spot to park them when they aren't in use can be a real headache. No matter where you leave them, they always seem to be in the way: pedals bruise shins, kickstands trip innocent passersby, and handlebars scratch the side of your car. And with each encounter your valuable bicycles suffer chipped paint or bent spokes.

With this clever bicycle rack, you can store up to four bicycles off the ground and out of the way. Pairs of sliding brackets mount onto the main frame, holding each bicycle so securely that you can even do maintenance work on it while it is in the rack. Because the brackets are padded, there is no risk of scratching the paint.

This bike rack does more than support bicycles for storage or service. It also features handy storage compartments at the base of the rack, so you can keep spoke wrenches and spare inner tubes right where you need them.

Because not all cyclists' needs are the same, we have designed this rack so you can modify it to meet your own storage needs. The design, as shown, will accommodate two adult-size and two children-size bicycles. But by simply making the rack posts 12" taller, you can store up to four full-size bicycles. However you decide to build it, this rack will allow you and your family to spend more time cycling and less time looking for parking spots at home.

CONSTRUCTION MATERIALS

Quantity	Lumber
6	2 × 4" × 8' pine
4	2 × 2" × 8' pine
2	2 × 10" × 8' pine
2	½" × 2' × 4' plywood

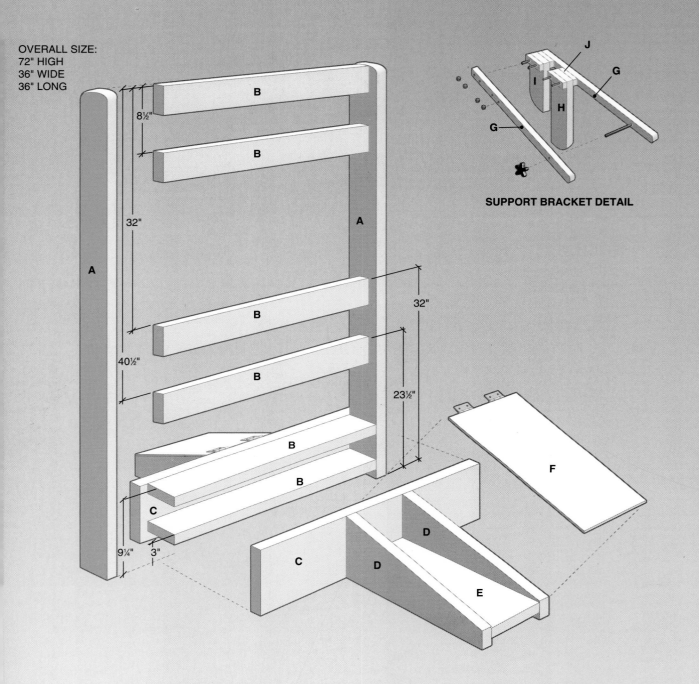

OVERALL SIZE:
72" HIGH
36" WIDE
36" LONG

SUPPORT BRACKET DETAIL

Cutting List

Key	Part	Dimension	Pcs.	Material
A	Post	1½ × 3½ × 72"	2	Pine
B	Cross rail	1½ × 3½ × 34½"	6	Pine
C	Cross brace	1½ × 9¼ × 37½"	2	Pine
D	Foot	1½ × 9¼ × 19¾"	4	Pine
E	Foot base	1½ × 9¼ × 19¾"	2	Pine

Cutting List

Key	Part	Dimension	Pcs.	Material
F	Cover	½ × 12¼ × 21"	2	Plywood
G	Bracket arm	1½ × 1½ × 20"	16	Pine
H	Bracket leg	1½ × 3½ × 13½"	8	Pine
I	Bracket leg	1½ × 3½ × 6½"	8	Pine
J	Bracket spacer	½ × 1½ × 8½"	8	Plywood

Materials: Glue, wood screws (#8 × 3", #8 × 2½"), ⅜"-dia. carriage bolts, nuts, washers, ⅜"-dia., 16 threads-per-inch plastic knobs (8), utility hinges (1½ × 1½"), closed-cell foam strips, finishing materials.

Note: Measurements reflect the actual size of dimensional lumber.

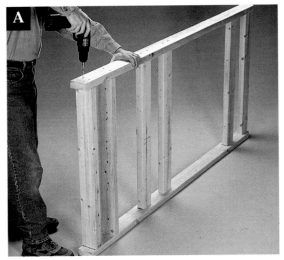
Attach the bottom pair of cross rails between the posts, with their broad faces up.

Use a circular saw to cut the tapered sides of the feet for the base.

Directions:
Family Bike Rack

BUILD THE MAIN FRAME. The main frame of this bike rack consists of two 6'-tall posts that support pairs of 2 × 4 cross rails. When the rack is completed, the upper pairs of rails will hold the brackets that support the bikes. Cut the posts (A) to length (see *Tip*, below), then round off the top ends with a jig saw and sand the curves smooth (a belt sander mounted to your worksurface on its side can be used to make the roundovers). Draw a centerline from top to bottom on the inside face of each post to use as a reference for positioning the cross rails. Cut the cross rails (B) and attach them between the posts with glue and #8 × 3" wood screws. The top four cross rails should be centered on the center-lines, with their broad faces pointing out. Attach the top rail flush with the tops of the posts; attach the second rail with its top edge 8½" down from the tops of the posts; attach the third rail with its top edge 32" down from the tops of the posts; attach the fourth rail with its top edge 40½" down from the tops of the posts. The two rails closest to the bottom should be fastened with their broad faces up. Attach them so the tops are 9¼" and 5" up from the bottoms of the posts **(photo A).**

BUILD THE BASE. The base for this bike rack provides support for the main frame, as well as storage for your tools and equipment. It features two tapered feet that extend out in

C

Attach the base assemblies to the posts and bottom cross rails on the main frame.

the front and back of the rack. The feet are attached to heavy 2 × 10 cross braces that fit around the lower cross rails. Cut the cross braces (C), feet (D) and foot bases (E) from 2 × 10 pine. Draw cutting lines on the sides of the feet for the tapers: mark a point on one end of each foot, 3" up from the bottom edge. Use a straight-edge to draw lines connecting

TIP

Add 12" to the height of each post if you want your bike rack to accommodate four adult-size bikes. Add the height at the bottom of the posts to raise the middle set of cross rails without affecting the distance between the upper and middle sets of rails.

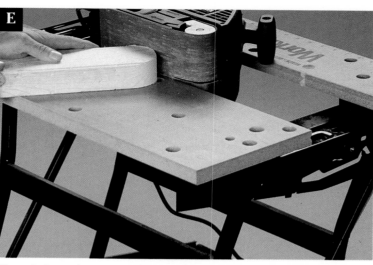

Attach hinged covers to the cross braces of the base to protect the storage space.

Use a belt sander mounted to your worksurface to smooth out the roundover cuts at the ends of the bracket legs.

the points with the top, opposite ends of each foot. Cut along each cutting line with a circular saw **(photo B).** Use glue and #8 × 3" wood screws to fasten a foot base between each pair of feet, with a 1½" gap between each base and the bottoms of the feet. Attach the foot assemblies to the cross braces, centered from end to end, by driving #8 × 3" screws through the cross braces and into the ends of the feet. Fasten the assemblies to the main frame by driving screws through the cross braces and into the posts and lower two cross rails **(photo C)**—use glue at all joints, and make sure the ends of the cross braces are flush with the outside faces of the posts. Cut the covers (F) for the feet from ½"-thick plywood, and mount them on the cross braces with utility hinges **(photo D).**

BUILD SUPPORT BRACKETS. The support brackets are essentially wooden clamps that slip over pairs of cross rails and hold the bicycles in place. Two brackets are needed to hold a bicycle: one bracket is clamped

to the seat post, and the other to the handlebar post. Cut the bracket arms (G), bracket legs (H, I), and bracket spacers (J). Use a compass set to a 1¾" radius to mark a full roundover on the ends of the taller bracket legs (H). Mark a 1¾"radius on one side only at the ends of the shorter bracket legs (I)—(see *Diagram,* page 93). Cut off the roundovers on all parts with a jig saw, then smooth them out on a belt sander mounted to your worksurface **(photo E).** Also round over one end of each arm slightly on the belt sander. Place a pair of arms on a flat worksurface so that the square ends are together. Position two spacers between them, flush with the square ends. Position one longer bracket leg and one shorter leg between the arms and spacers. The back edge of the shorter leg should be flush with the square ends of the arms (see photo G), and the longer leg should be 1½" from the shorter leg (to fit over the 1½"-thick rails). Once you have the pieces in correct position, clamp them together. Drill ⅜"-dia. guide holes for carriage

bolts through the arms, spacers and legs. Space the guide holes for evenly spaced bolts at each leg location **(photo F).** Unclamp the parts, apply glue and fasten the bracket parts together with carriage bolts, washers and nuts. Insert a 2 × 4 spacer between the free ends of the arms, and drill a ⅜"-dia. hole through both arms, 4" in from the ends of the arms **(photo G).** This hole is for the carriage bolts used to draw the arms together around the bicycle frame. Insert a carriage bolt through the arms (remove the spacer) so the head is tight against the outside face of one arm. Slip a washer over the free end of the carriage bolt, and twist a threaded knob (⅜"-dia.) on the end. By turning the knob, you can draw the arms together (there is enough flex in 2 × 2 pine to make this happen). Repeat these steps for all the support brackets.

> TIP
>
> *For balance and trouble-free storage, arrange bicycles so they point in opposite directions when sharing a pair of cross rails. If your bicycle has pedals that remove easily, take them off before storage. If security is a concern, you can lock your bicycle to the rack.*

Drill ⅜"-dia. guide holes for carriage bolts through the arms, brackets and spacers.

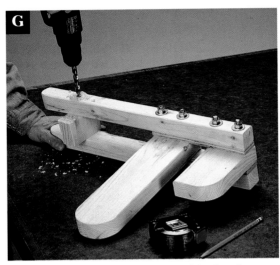

With a spacer between the ends of the bracket arms, drill a ⅜"-dia. guide hole through the arms for the bolt that draws the arm ends together.

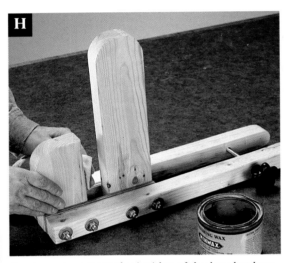

Apply paste wax to the insides of the bracket legs, and to the main-frame rails as a lubricant.

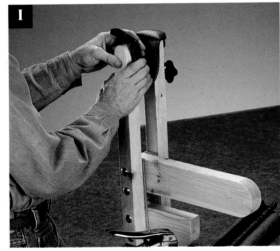

Staple closed-cell foam strips onto the ends of the bracket arms to protect the bike frame.

APPLY FINISHING TOUCHES. Sand all the surfaces with medium (100- or 120-grit) sandpaper to smooth out rough spots, then finish-sand with fine (150- or 180-grit) sandpaper. Apply a finish to all the surfaces—we used two coats of polyurethane. Glossy enamel paint is also a good choice if you want a more finished appearance. Apply two or three coats of paste wax to the cross rails and the inside edges of the leg braces, buffing each coat until it is hardened **(photo H).** This will allow for easier movement of the braces. Cut pieces of thin (⅜ to ½"-thick) closed-cell foam to fit over the ends of the arms on the brackets. Staple the foam onto the ends to protect the bicycle frame **(photo I).** To use the bike rack, slip pairs of brackets over the top cross rail in each pair in the main frame. The cross rail should fit between the bracket legs. Test each bracket to make sure it is secure, then adjust the positions of the brackets so they align with the seat post and handlebar post of your bike. Lift the bike up so the posts fit between the ends of the arm pairs in each bracket, then tighten the star-shaped knob at the ends of each arm pair until the bike posts are held securely between the arms.